Dedication

To my three beautiful children, Joy, Jimmy, and Faith, in appreciation for their understanding and patience while my time was consumed by this project.

Acknowledgements

I would like to thank the following people: My publisher, Mark Gilroy, for believing in the vision for this project; my editing assistant, Kelly Wells, without whom this book could not have been completed; my editors, Jeff Dunn and Christina Honea for their exhaustive work on this project; my publicist, Cathy Tuttle, for her tireless promotion of my books (and me); my agent, Chip MacGregor, for his encouragement and enthusiasm.

Table of Contents

Introduction

As a financial planner and seminar teacher, I have come to the realization that many people can experience an almost overnight change in their financial circumstances by applying just a few simple principles. I know that anyone making such a claim would understandably be questioned. In fact, the idea that a few simple financial strategies can almost immediately change a person's life goes against all logic and common sense. This type of claim may be considered by many to be no different than a fad diet or a get-rich-quick scheme. After all, we have been told for our entire lives that building wealth and improving our finances is something that takes an entire lifetime.

The good news for you is that this is not the "10-Day Financial Plan," but *The 10-Day Financial Breakthrough.* A breakthrough is an event that catapults an individual's progress rapidly and immediately. It is like being in a dark room when someone suddenly turns on the lights. This book is designed to give you the necessary knowledge that can literally cut years off your journey to financial independence. Methods are explained in such a way as to revolutionize your thinking using the "90/10 principle." As a first-degree black belt in Tae Kwon Do, I have found that 90 percent of what I know about self-defense I learned the very first week. The basic elements of self-defense can be learned in just three or four lessons. The rest is practice, practice, practice. It's true in the area of finances as well. In only ten days you will be exposed to information that will immediately change your financial circumstances and give you results quicker than ever before.

Will you be a financial expert after just ten days? Most likely, no, but that is not the goal. *The 10-Day Financial Breakthrough* will explain the 90 percent that you *need to know* and—most importantly—will tell you *what to do* about your finances. This 90 percent impact can completely and totally revolutionize your financial future. I know it may sound hard to believe, but it can happen almost instantly—once you begin.

How to Use This Book

The 10-Day Financial Breakthrough is not a book that you *read*, but a book that you *do*. It is a plan to uncover your hidden wealth—a plan that you absolutely *can do* in ten days. Each day is filled with lists, charts, graphs, helps, and all kinds of action-oriented information. The most exciting thing about this book is the accompanying Web site, www.tenday.com, where you will find ongoing interactive assistance for your ten day journey. You will be able to download important forms and documents necessary for your financial breakthrough. The site also conveniently provides you with links to all of the Web addresses referenced in this book. You will find the password to access the site on page 163. I have hidden it on that page so only those people who read the book will have access to the Web site. This may seem unfair, but the Web site and the book go hand-in-hand. They are a team—like Abbott and Costello, peanut butter and jelly, and Tom and Jerry.

The Internet has allowed me to turbo-charge my best ideas and give you a way of getting virtually instant results. You may not own a home computer, but almost every public library in America now has at least one computer with an Internet connection. The Internet will allow you to go on my "Fast Track Plan" and easily complete your entire *10-Day Financial Breakthrough* on time—in some cases in even less than ten days!

This book is about getting you financially on track in the least amount of time possible. I am also committed to keeping you on track, which is why I have created a "Sustaining the Breakthrough" annual schedule.

Sustaining the breakthrough will require ongoing effort—using what you have learned—that will keep you on the right track throughout the year.

HELP ALONG THE WAY

You will find six different types of sidebars within this book. The following sidebar topics will give those of you who are speed-readers a way to digest ten days' worth of reading into one (although you won't be able to do everything in one day).

Christian Money Principle—While I am not presenting an in-depth Bible study, as a Christian I am basing my advice on biblical principles. When you see this graphic, you will know I am offering you an important spiritual insight.

Fast Track—If you don't have time to read all of that boring financial stuff, OK. This is for you. When you see this graphic you will be getting to the "what-to-do" section for that day. Fast Track is the express lane of my financial supermarket. Follow the Fast Track icons, and you will know what to do right away.

Internet Time Savers—When you see this graphic you will know that it is time to click on your computer and get on the Internet. If you don't have Internet access at home, use a friend's computer or go to a library and use one for free. You will miss out on much of what this book can do for you if you don't combine it with the power of the Internet.

Get to the Point—If you just want "the bottom line," look for this graphic and skip the longer presentation. This graphic is designed to give you the most important points.

Money Talk—This graphic will help define what I affectionately call "technobabble." Here I'll explain a fancy word that some number-cruncher made up just to confuse you.

Cashing In—Hey! You paid good money for this book and are going to skip TV for the next ten nights to go through it, so you should expect some kind of reward. When you see this graphic, you will learn what the financial payoff is for completing that day's tasks.

Day 1

Define Your Financial Goals

S	M	T	W	T	F	S
	①1	2	3	4	5	6

✔ This is the first day of your financial breakthrough. Each day will take you through a different aspect of gaining control of your finances. Today, you are going to find out what your financial condition really is. Don't jump to conclusions—you may be surprised! Also, you will learn how to set financial goals to get where you want to be. In order to reach your goals, you will need to know how to design a plan to get you there.

WHAT YOU WILL NEED:

- Recent bank statements and checkbook ledgers.
- Recent investment statements.
- Value estimates on all personal property and real estate.
- Loan statements and financial records to establish how much debt you currently have.

- Time for a family meeting, to make sure your goals are similar to those of your spouse. If you are single, time to talk about your finances with someone you trust.

YOUR "BREAKTHROUGH I.Q."

Cashing In

The amount of financial benefit you and your family will derive from setting financial goals can be enormous. On average, an individual with a four-year college degree in today's economy will earn one million dollars more during their career than without it! Did you know that saving $100 per month from the time your child is born can provide $40,000 for that child's college education? What about a twenty-five year-old who saves $21 per week? By the time he reaches the age of sixty-five he should have more than one million dollars accumulated. A million here, a million there—today we are dealing with real money.

Answer the following questions as accurately as you can, using the five-point system to rate your responses. If you strongly agree with the statement, give yourself a 5. If you strongly disagree with the statement, or it is false, score a 1. Take this question, for example: "Do you have a consistent monthly savings plan for your children's college fund?" If your answer is "No, I haven't thought about that yet," then circle the 1 (the lowest). If you sporadically save for their college, select 3 (mid level). On the other hand, if you are making regular monthly contributions, select 5 (highest level).

FINANCIAL-EVALUATION QUIZ

I know what my net worth is (my assets less my debts).   1 2 3 4 5

I have specific written financial goals for my retirement (exact amounts you are working to accumulate).   1 2 3 4 5

I have specific written goals for funding my other financial goals (college education for children, dream home, etc.).   1 2 3 4 5

I do not regularly carry balances on my credit cards (5 points if you do not carry balances and fewer points if you do).   1 2 3 4 5

I have evaluated my life insurance needs and have a plan that will take care of my responsibilities in the event of my death.   1 2 3 4 5

I have a valid will and have evaluated whether I also need a living trust.   1 2 3 4 5

I have a written budget that I generally follow.   1 2 3 4 5

I have a financial management system (such as financial software) that I use to monitor my spending.   1 2 3 4 5

I am taking full advantage of my retirement plan opportunities (IRAs, 401Ks, etc.).   1 2 3 4 5

I understand the investments that I am making and am confident that they will earn enough for me to reach my financial goals.   1 2 3 4 5

I am confident that I am being paid what I am worth and have taken advantage of opportunities to increase my earning potential.   1 2 3 4 5

I have shopped insurance rates in the last twelve months to be sure I have the best deal.   1 2 3 4 5

I know that I am adequately insured (which means that if I am in a car accident or a visitor is hurt in my home I would be protected for at least one million dollars).   1 2 3 4 5

I understand all of the insurance coverage that I am buying and am convinced that I need it and do not have any duplicate coverage.   1 2 3 4 5

I have a plan to control my tax liability and am taking full advantage of the tax deductions available to me.   1 2 3 4 5

Your Total Score

YOUR BREAKTHROUGH I.Q.

60 or higher: You are on the right track and are well above 95 percent of Americans.

50 to 59: You have a basic grasp of your finances, but can make major improvements.

40 to 49: You are about average, as most Americans don't do much financial planning.

less than 40: Don't be too hard on yourself. (After all, you bought this book, right?)

Money Talk

Financial goals are simply specific financial objectives you desire to reach.

GOAL SETTING

The topic of goal setting is a tired concept to say the least. If you have attended any motivational seminar or read any success book, you have undoubtedly heard the mantra of why goal setting is the key to getting ahead in life. The problem with getting excited and spouting out your fantasies is that this approach will not do anything but give you a temporary exhilaration. After a day or two, you will be back to the daily grind and will only have faint memories of the dreams you had. In order to produce the results you want, your goals must be realistic, specific, and measurable. A good friend of mine who taught me much of what I know about money, the late Charles Givens, described goals as "a dream with a deadline." I love that definition because it moves us beyond the fantasy and challenges us to get specific.

Today will be the most important day of your financial breakthrough, but not just because it is the first day and you are beginning your journey. This is the most important day because you, and only you, will be making specific financial plans for the rest of your life. Financial planning is really a very simple process at its core. It is true that experts can help you along the way, but the first and most powerful step is to figure out where you are presently. The second is to determine where you want to be in the future.

WHY PEOPLE DON'T SET GOALS

People fail to set goals for different reasons. Mine was that I thought goal setting and making plans was silly—until I tried it. When I was young and fresh out of school, I thought I was going to enjoy a career in real estate, but I was absolutely

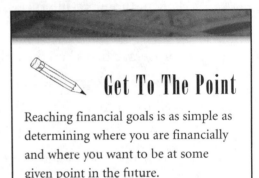

Get To The Point

Reaching financial goals is as simple as determining where you are financially and where you want to be at some given point in the future.

miserable. One of the first jobs I had was working in a real estate development. I was not very excited about the whole idea of showing houses. The development did not even have a model home to put me in, so I was stuck in a mobile home. Most of the day, I would sit and wait for a prospect to walk in the door. Some days no one would come in at all. With all that free time on my hands, I did some serious thinking. While sitting in that dusty old trailer, I decided that I wanted to become a stockbroker. I set a goal.

I pulled out a phone book and started calling every brokerage firm in town. They all told me the same sad news: They were not hiring. Despite an obvious lack of opportunity, I sheepishly told my wife about my stockbroker idea. Ann said she'd stand by me. (I am blessed to have a wife who has always been supportive of me, even when it was not rational to do so.) After her encouraging response, I became completely obsessed with the idea. But the more phone calls I made, the more brick walls I ran into. I purchased a map of Florida and determined what distance would represent a one-hour commute from our tiny home in Kissimmee.

In those pre-Internet days, I had to go to the library to get the phone books for these communities and make a list of all of the brokerage firms and their phone numbers. I was encouraged since I now had a larger field of prospects to call, and after calling (and calling!) I finally hit pay dirt. A firm in Orlando offered me an interview. The good news: I was offered a job. The bad news: There was a catch (actually a few). I would be given no salary, no leads, and had to go to a training seminar in Colorado for a month. I shared with my wife this wonderful "opportunity," and again she gave me the green light. It was incredible. My wife was willing to back me 100 percent in addition to agreeing to earn all of our income for the next two years.

But there was still one small problem. I needed two thousand dollars to take the training and to pay for everything involved with earning my securities license, and I had no way of getting it. I thought long and hard and prayed. The Lord brought to mind Maxine Kiely, the lady who sold me my condominium. I had heard that in addition to real estate, she worked with a bank. I called her for help, and in one week she had a $2,000 loan approved for me. I was completely amazed. My story began with a depressed guy sitting in a mobile home who set a goal. The rest is history.

You may have noticed that it was not just me—or the goal—that caused the change. What made the difference was community. People will get behind you when they learn that you are striving to accomplish something. The other key is God. He will open doors when we are pursuing the dreams He places in our hearts.

THE COMPONENTS OF SUCCESSFUL GOAL SETTING

Vague goals are of no value. The more specific you are when you set goals, the higher the probability that you will achieve them. I have met people at my seminars who were so frustrated working out their goals I was convinced that they wanted to

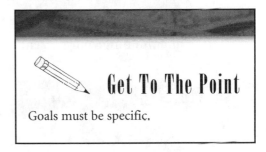

Get To The Point
Goals must be specific.

punch me in the nose. The frustration stems from the fact that most people have never set a specific goal and wouldn't know how if they had to. On the issue of retirement, for example, many people say, "Someday I would like to have a nice retirement." While this may be wishful thinking, it is not a goal because it lacks any specifics. I challenge my seminar students to get as specific as possible. Many times the

Get To The Point
Your financial goals must be your own.

reaction is "OK Jim. Then *you* tell me what my goals should be." It just doesn't work that way.

I will not, and realistically cannot, set your financial goals for you (nor can anyone else). This is a highly personal process that each individual must do on his own—or, at most, with his or her spouse. For most of us, it is easy to imagine a day when we have financial independence—the ability to do away with the 9-to-5 routine in exchange for other pursuits (volunteer work, missions, spoiling grandchildren, hobbies, etc.). We can easily picture the things we would enjoy when that day arrives. Putting all this down on paper and making it specific becomes the problem. There are a number of ways to do this. One way is to determine the lump sum of money you will need (think of a sum that would enable you to retire from your job, while maintaining your current level of income). A second approach is to shoot for a monthly or annual income amount and then work backward to get the lump sum amount. Later on I will discuss with you in detail how to work out these numbers in conjunction with an investment plan. You may also wish to check out the retirement calculator service available at www.christianmoney.com.

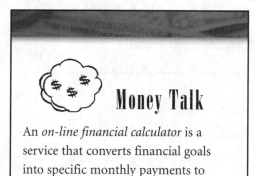

Money Talk

An *on-line financial calculator* is a service that converts financial goals into specific monthly payments to reach them.

DETERMINING YOUR NET WORTH

(This form may be downloaded at www.tenday.com.)

Name(s)	Date
Assets	**Current Value**

Liquid Assets

Certificates of Deposit　　　　_____

Savings Accounts　　　　_____

Checking Accounts　　　　_____

Bank Money-Market Accounts　　　　_____

Mutual Fund Money-Market Funds　　　　_____

Cash on Hand　　　　_____

Taxable Securities

Individual Stocks　　　　_____

Individual Bonds　　　　_____

Stock Mutual Funds　　　　_____

Bond Mutual Funds　　　　_____

Other (Futures, Options, etc.)　　　　_____

Retirement Plans

Individual Retirement Accounts (IRAs)　　_____

SEP-IRAs　　　　_____

Keogh Plans　　　　_____

401(k) Plans　　　　_____

403(b) Plans　　　　_____

457 Plans　　　　_____

Annuities   _____

Other   _____

Life Insurance   **Current Value**

Life Insurance Cash Value   _____

Real Estate

Primary Residence   _____

Other Home(s)   _____

Rental Property   _____

Real Estate Investment Trusts (REITs)   _____

Real Estate Limited Partnerships   _____

Personal Property

Antiques   _____

Appliances   _____

Autos   _____

Boats   _____

Clothing   _____

Computers   _____

Furnishings   _____

Jewelry   _____

Tools   _____

TVs, VCRs, Stereos, etc.   _____

Other Property   _____

Total Assets   _____

Liabilities

Installment Loans	**Balance (Amount Owed)**
Automobiles	_____
Appliances	_____
Furniture	_____

Mortgage Loans	**Balance (Amount Owed)**
Primary Residence	_____
Secondary Residence(s)	_____
Other Property	_____

Additional Loans

Unsecured (credit cards, lines of credit, etc.)	_____
Secured Loans	_____
Other	_____

Total Liabilities	_____

Once you've calculated your total assets as well as your total liabilities, it's time to do some subtraction:

_____ – _____ = _____

    Total Assets   Total Liabilities   Current Net Worth

Notice that in the calculation above, the words "net worth" are preceded by the word "current." Your net worth is not a static figure but, rather, one that will change as your financial profile changes. Do yourself a favor and update your net worth statement frequently. You should also make a copy of these calculations and store this record with your other valuable documents.

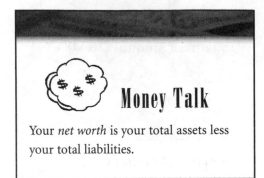

Money Talk

Your *net worth* is your total assets less your total liabilities.

By determining your current net worth you are finding the starting point of your financial journey. Although this seems like a very simple exercise, I am convinced that most people have never done it. Imagine how difficult it would be to improve your finances without knowing the details of your current financial situation. Now that you know where you are, let's move on to the matter of deciding on a future destination.

HOW TO LIST YOUR FINANCIAL GOALS

As I have shared with you, goals are a very personal matter. Consequently, it would be impossible for me to set financial goals for you or anyone else for that matter. So where do you begin? Sit down and think about what you want and also what you need. It is important to understand the difference between "wants" and "needs." That said, it is perfectly fine to include "wants" in your financial goals. Goals based on needs might include money for retirement or your children's college fund. On the other hand, you might also want to take a special vacation or purchase a recreational vehicle.

Use the chart below to list some goals that are important to you. I encourage you to take the time to write down your goals because it is a simple way of making a commitment to achieve them. Talking about accomplishing something is one thing. Deciding to write it down really speaks to how resolute you are about reaching it. The goal selection is up to you. Later, I will show you how to break that goal down into a financial figure and how to create a plan to achieve it.

LIST YOUR FINANCIAL GOALS

1. _____
2. _____
3. _____
4. _____
5. _____
6. _____
7. _____
8. _____
9. _____
10. _____

MAKING YOUR GOALS HAPPEN

Now that you have written down some financial goals, you have taken the first step toward making your goals happen. The next step, however, is equally important. Now you must reconcile your goals with reality. For example, you may indicate on your goal list that you want to retire with a million dollars in savings. Your ability to actually realize that goal, however, will depend largely on your current age, your income, and the amount of savings you've accumulated thus far. If you are twenty-four years old and you earn a decent living, one that permits you to set aside at least $100 a month, your goal is certainly achievable. If, however, you are fifty-seven years old, you earn $30,000 a year and have no retirement savings thus far, it's probably not reasonable to presume that you will be able to achieve that goal.

EXAMPLES OF FINANCIAL GOALS

Goal	Amount Required	Savings You Have Now	Monthly Savings Required
College/child	$75,000	$10,000	$273 for 14 years
New Boat	$20,000	$5,000	$204 for 4 years
Retirement	$1,000,000	$50,000	$144 per month

Money Talk

A *financial calculator* can be purchased for about $25. These special calculators make it easier to calculate what amount you need to save each month to reach your financial goals.

I deliberately gave the example of a boat for my male readers. It also gives me a chance to say your financial goals can include items such as a boat, a recreational vehicle, a special vacation, or other such extravagance. It is perfectly fine to treat yourself with these kinds of purchases so long as you do so within the context of your overall plan. Before you rush out and buy a boat, let me emphasize that in the example above the boat is to be purchased *after* the money is saved. Setting this type of financial goal is not an excuse to go into debt. It also should not take money away from your goals based on *needs,* such as your retirement or college funding for your children.

Life is a balancing act, and completely depriving yourself is not necessary or healthy. I find that just like most fad diets, many people will starve themselves and then go out and binge. Financially, that may parallel going out and buying a boat or some other item that is way out of the budget. They can't afford it, because they didn't plan.

WHAT FINANCIAL CALCULATORS CAN DO

I recommend that you consider investing in a financial calculator. This is a hand-held calculator that looks like any other, but it includes additional functions that allow you to account for the time value of money (the effects of compounding, if you will). This instrument will help provide valuable information about reaching your goals. For example, it will enable you to answer such questions as how much money you'll need to set aside each month in an investment that earns 10 percent a year in order to have $10,000 at the end of 12 years. Only a financial calculator can solve those kinds of problems for you easily and quickly.

While many of you may find it easier to use the online calculators available at various sites on the Internet as well as www.tenday.com, you can do some amazing calculations with a simple handheld unit. Some of the calculations include mortgage payments (and prepayment scenarios), college or retirement savings, and even more complex calculations such as internal rates of return.

MONITORING YOUR FINANCIAL PROGRESS

An important final step in the process of goal setting is ongoing monitoring of your progress. If you skip a month here and there or if your investments don't earn what you expected, you may have to make adjustments from time to time. I suggest that at least once or twice per year you take inventory of where you are in relation to your financial goals. These frequent evaluations will give you the opportunity to adjust your course as needed.

INTERNET TIME SAVERS

www.christianmoney.com—I offer a service called Christian Money Net. The service provides a host of benefits for $9.95 per month. Among the benefits are unlimited use of my retirement, college funding, and life insurance calculators. These calculators are unique since they are not automated. I personally perform each calculation and e-mail the answer, usually with a few bonus comments.

Other great financial sites with lots of resources and retirement calculator-type services as well:

General

www.moneycentral.com—MSN Money Central

www.quicken.com—Quicken also has money-management software.

www.kiplinger.com—Official Web site for Kiplinger.

Investments

www.vanguard.com—Official Web site for Vanguard.

www.estrong.com—Official Web site for Strong Funds.

Other sites of interest

www.ssa.gov—Official Web site for the Social Security Administration. Request a copy of your Social Security statement on-line.

www.collegesavings.org—Official Web site for the National Association of State Treasurers. Receive help with college funding and planning.

FAST TRACK

1. Your financial breakthrough begins by establishing goals for the future.
2. Financial goals must be specific. Vague goals cannot be used to create a plan of action.
3. Specific goals must be converted into an action plan. For example, how much money will you need to save each month to fund your retirement or your children's college education?
4. Purchase a financial calculator so that you can do your own time value of money computations.
5. If you don't want to purchase a financial calculator, you can use an on-line calculator service (see Internet Time Savers for this chapter).

DAY 1 DIARY

I am on my way to my financial breakthrough. Today I . . .

_____

_____

_____

_____

_____

_____

_____

_____

_____

_____

_____

_____

_____

_____

_____

_____

_____

_____

Day 2

Build A Budget

S	M	T	W	T	F	S
1		②	3	4	5	6

✔ You are now beginning the second day of your financial breakthrough. Now that you have established some financial goals, today you will learn how to get the most from your monthly income. You will learn how to successfully manage your monthly income and expenditures using a budget and how to find "extra money."

WHAT YOU WILL NEED:

- Your checkbook ledger for at least one year or preferably a printout of your checking account from a software program like Quicken or Microsoft Money.

- A list of your ongoing expenses items. This includes "bills," but involves much more. For example, you do not receive a bill for your monthly haircuts but need to include this in your budget.

CHRISTIAN MONEY PRINCIPLE

Go to the ant, you sluggard; consider its ways and be wise! It has no commander, no overseer or ruler, yet it stores its provisions in summer and gathers its food at harvest.

—Proverbs 6:6-8

It doesn't matter what financial book you read or success system you follow, every road that leads to financial freedom is paved with money that is left over after all of the bills are paid each month. This "extra money" is what I will refer to as your "financial surplus." If having money left over is really the road to financial success, what is the road to financial destruction? You guessed it: Spending more than you earn each month. It is easy to accurately forecast your financial future based on how you manage your finances during the course of a one-month period. If you are not saving money *this* month, chances are you do not save regularly. It is even more likely that you have accumulated several "overspending" months and are now substantially in debt. If you outspend your income *this* month, it is likely that this has happened during other months as well. Your habits *this* month most likely reflect your financial lifestyle.

Our time on earth is simply a series of days . . . that make up months . . . that turn into years . . . and then decades. It can be a scary proposition to look forward ten or even twenty years from now. You may wonder how you are going to reach your goals. The exciting news is that anyone can commit to a financial plan just *one month at a time.* After a string of successful months, soon you will have been on track for a year. Before long you will have successfully managed your plan for a few years and so on. This is really the simple secret of financial success.

If you can get it in your mind that a behavior practiced well in one month can become a habit for a lifetime, then you are about to develop the blueprint for your entire financial success. Your one-month financial plan, which you can call a "budget spending plan" or any term you desire, is the foundation to building substantial wealth during your lifetime and becoming debt free.

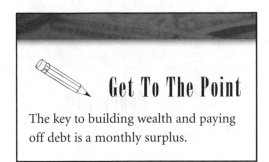

Get To The Point

The key to building wealth and paying off debt is a monthly surplus.

LIVING WITHIN A BUDGET

The idea of living on a budget is not a popular one. The thought of "cutting back" is just not an exciting proposition for most people. The reason why budgets get such a negative rap is that the concept is presented in the wrong light. A budget is not about *doing without,* but being able to *have* the things that you want. Within the context of a solid plan, it really is possible to live

Cashing In

Living on a budget is perhaps the most fundamental step in all of financial planning. After all, it is the success of your budget that will determine if you have money left over (your surplus) to invest, or if you will join the millions who spend more than they make. The key to financial success is actually very simple: Spend less than you earn for a long period of time. Once you are sticking to a budget, use 50 percent of your savings (the amount you are not spending) to invest with the goal of doubling your money every six to seven years. Use the other 50 percent to pay toward your debt.

Money Talk

A *budget* is a monthly spending plan that guides your daily spending.

your financial dreams. We have all known people who seem constantly to be getting ahead financially, despite having a modest income. They earn less money than you, but still manage to take wonderful vacations. They are always beautifully dressed in the latest fashions. They even seem to take an occasional overnight escape with their spouse to a five-star resort. To top it all off, they have one of those shiny foreign sports cars. What gives?

Would you be surprised to learn the following?

- Their clothing was bought at discount stores and factory direct outlets (and even some of it from consignment shops).
- They purchased their car for cash and bought it at wholesale by going to a local auto auction.
- They plan their vacations a year in advance and use the Internet to get up to 70 percent off the regular price.
- They look for specials and tap into those "name-your-own-price sites" to stay at world class resorts for the price of a budget motel.

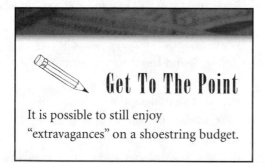

Get To The Point

It is possible to still enjoy "extravagances" on a shoestring budget.

These people are resourceful and make their money go further than those who won't take the time to find the deals. The analogy that I use in my seminars is that of a car. We all have owned "gas-guzzlers" that seem to run out of gas by the time we are a block away from filling up. There are also the smaller more fuel-efficient cars that seem to never run out of gas. I rented one such car on a business trip and drove it for three days and used less than one-quarter of a tank. Now that's a financial breakthrough! You can choose to be a money guzzler and go through your money like one of those giant paramilitary vehicles (otherwise known as SUVs) goes through gas. On the other hand, you can become a sixty-mile-per-gallon economy car. You see, in either vehicle you can travel the same speed and still get to the same destination. The cost of doing so is based solely on the choice that you make. A budget is simply your plan to get what you want within the constraints of the amount of money that you have to do it. Doesn't that sound more exciting than what you normally hear about budgets?

What if it were possible to convince other people to help you meet your budget goals? Most often we think of budgeting as *our* cutting back and learning to live without. What if we could get the following people to "chip in" to help you meet your budget goals:

> ### Get To The Point
>
> "Cutting back" also includes saving money by reducing the cost of your financial services such as mortgage rates, insurance rates, credit cards, and more.

- Your banker
- Your stockbroker
- Your insurance agent(s)
- Your credit card company(s)
- Your mortgage lender

Simply call them and explain that you are now on a budget and need them to cut back their fees. A bad idea? Who could imagine doing such a thing, and what would these people say (after they stop laughing)? Believe it or not, this is what you are going to learn to do as part of today's breakthrough. You will learn how to reduce the amount you are paying to all of these people and whether they know it or not, they will be reducing their bill to help you meet your budget.

What about cutting back, doing without, taking the brown bag lunch, eating hot dogs instead of steak? Where does all of that come in?

Get To The Point

Living on a budget means making choices and setting priorities.

It would be disingenuous of me not to inform you that part of the equation is learning to cut back. Life is a tradeoff. Maybe you will "brown bag it" this week and use the money to catch that popular movie on Friday night. Perhaps you can do without that new golf club and instead buy a used one at your local sports consignment shop for 80 percent less. You could use the savings to play two extra rounds of golf this month. (Now that's a strategy!)

The following are some crazy and unbelievable bargains I have personally witnessed:

- Individuals volunteer as "air couriers." They give up their luggage space in the plane and in exchange they get 95 percent off their airfare (learn how to do this in Christian Money Net at www.christianmoney.com).
- A client of mine lives three months out of the year at Yosemite National Park. How much does he pay to do this? Nothing. He gets paid to do this as a seasonal park ranger!
- Some local families regularly go to "kids-eat-free nights" in town. They eat out several nights a week for less than it would cost to buy the food and prepare it at home (and they don't have to do the dishes).
- Friends take last-minute cruises and pay as little as $400 for two people to go on a four-day cruise!

These are just a few examples of bargains available for the finding. It really is possible to have the things that are important to you—and still follow a budget.

IS THERE A BLUEPRINT FOR YOUR BUDGET?

Get To The Point

No two budgets are exactly alike.

I have read books that seem to imply that there are appropriate percentages for clothing or housing or other spending categories that apply equally to all people. However, I believe these are really personal lifestyle issues. For example, if you are single, you would likely spend a greater percentage of your income on entertainment and recreation than a married person. These issues are also affected by regional implications. Many people who live in and near major cities do not purchase automobiles, but rely on public transportation. These and other unique considerations make it difficult to put individuals into categories and tell them specifically how their money should be allocated dollar for dollar.

FUNDAMENTALS OF BUDGETING

Although no two budgets are alike, there are some basic rules that must be approached uniformly. First of all, you must include all of your monthly expense items in your list of expenditures, or you will be unsuccessful. Many people only think of "bills" when they begin to list their expenses. Of course, the cable company, electric company, and other businesses that you have accounts with will all send you a monthly bill. These items are a part of your budget, but are not the entire picture. Also included should be incidentals such as eating out, gas, clothing, groceries, etc. Additionally, you must remember the most important premise of budgeting—you cannot spend more than your income.

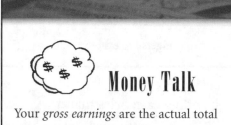

Money Talk

Your *gross earnings* are the actual total money that your employer owes you, prior to deductions for taxes and Social Security. *Net* is the term used for your "take-home" pay.

Many people have little or no idea of what their true monthly income is. Although that may seem very questionable, it is surprisingly common how many of my clients *believe* they have more money coming in than they do. This can be as simple as basing their belief on their "gross" and not their "net take home pay." It is also the product of what I call "optimistic rounding." The way this works is that you round *up* your income and round *down* your expenses. This makes you *feel* better about your circumstances—for the moment.

For example, if you earn $3,000 per month (which is $36,000 per year) you may state (and actually believe) that you are earning $40,000 per year (rounding up). If a mortgage payment were $2,200, most people would say it was "$2,000." In order for your budget to work, you *must* use exact figures. This would be a good time to stop and decide where you are going to get your financial data. The easiest method would be to rely on a printout of your actual expenses from a financial management software program such as Quicken or Microsoft Money. If you are not using a system like this, you will need to accumulate your checkbook ledgers for at least six months (preferably one year).

When completing your monthly
listing of expenditures, don't forget to
also include money for items that
come up quarterly or annually. The
best way to handle these kinds of
expenses is to list one-twelfth of the
amount as a part of your monthly
outflow. For example, if you make an
annual real estate tax payment of
$2,400 you should list this as $200 in
your monthly budget. Until the taxes
actually come due, the money should be set aside in a separate account.
If you are saving toward a vacation or special occasion, do so by saving
a little each month until you reach your goal.

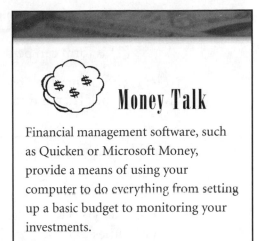

Money Talk

Financial management software, such
as Quicken or Microsoft Money,
provide a means of using your
computer to do everything from setting
up a basic budget to monitoring your
investments.

DETERMINING YOUR MONTHLY CASH FLOW

(This form can be downloaded at www.tenday.com.)

Note: If you do not have exact figures, just estimate for now. You can always go back later and make adjustments.

Name(s)_____ Date _____

Monthly Income	**Amount**
Salary	_____
Bonuses	_____
Commissions	_____
Gratuities	_____
Royalties	_____
Part-Time Employment	_____
Self-Employed Income	_____
Interest from Investments	_____
Dividends from Investments	_____
Alimony	_____
Child Support	_____
Unemployment Compensation	_____
Disability	_____
Trust Income	_____
Worker's Compensation	_____
Social Security	_____
Income from Retirement Plans	_____
Total Monthly Income	_____

Monthly Expenses	**Amount**
Mortgage/Rent	_____
Groceries	_____
Electricity	_____
Water	_____
Telephone	_____
Other Utilities	_____

Auto Payments   _____
Auto-Related Expenses   _____
Life Insurance   _____
Health Insurance   _____
Homeowner's Insurance   _____
Auto Insurance   _____
Other Insurance   _____
Credit Card Payments   _____
Other Loan Payments   _____
Education   _____
Child Care   _____
Clothing   _____
Personal Grooming   _____
Cable Television   _____
Entertainment   _____
Gifts (Non-Charitable)   _____
Charitable Giving (includes church)   _____
Laundry   _____
Alimony   _____
Child Support   _____
Contributions to Savings   _____
Contributions to Taxable Investments   _____
Contributions to Retirement Plans   _____
Miscellaneous   _____
Federal Income Taxes   _____
State Income Taxes   _____
Municipal Taxes   _____
Property Taxes   _____
Other Taxes   _____
Other Expenses   _____
Total Monthly Expenses   _____

_____ – _____ = _____
Total Monthly Income   **Total Monthly Expenses**   **Monthly Surplus**

You did end up with a surplus, didn't you? If not, review your budget for areas where you can reduce spending. Do not try to just break even. You will need a surplus to help you build wealth and achieve true financial freedom.

Just because you have positive cash flow on paper does not mean you will have real money left at the end of the month. I strongly recommend that you take great care with your income and expense amounts. This will be absolutely critical to your *10-Day Financial Breakthrough*. Once you have set up your budget you will need to put in place a method of monitoring your progress and a system that will prevent you from overspending. One such approach that is very popular is known as the "envelope system." The idea is that you create an envelope for each of your spending categories and then place the money for that expense in the appropriate envelope. If you place $200 in your entertainment envelope, you can only spend money on entertainment until the envelope is empty and then you must stop for that month. While I like these "systems," and there are many of them, they do not deal with the fundamental problem that prevents most people from having a successful budget. You must find a way to be motivated to stay on your budget. If you find your best motivation is a reward (such as a special trip), build that into your budget too.

It is also critical that you find a motivation for your spouse and family to stick to the budget as well. All too often I get letters from people who want to know what to do about their spouse who refuses to stick to the family budget. It must be a team effort, and in order for it to work, your spouse must be involved in the process of formulating the budget in the first place. If you are married it is critical that both you and your spouse catch the vision and see the benefit of living within your budget. It will not work in the long run for one spouse to impose a budget on the other. It must be a team project, and compromise is the key.

🕐 INTERNET TIME SAVERS

On-line Help for Developing a Budget

www.christianmoney.com

www.tenday.com

www.crown.org—Official Web site for Larry Burkett.

www.daveramsey.com—Official Web site for Dave Ramsey.

www.quicken.com.saving.debt—Quicken Debt Reduction Planner.

www.dca.org—Official Web site for Debt Counselors of America.

www.financenter.com

www.shareware.com—Find free and low cost budgeting software.

www.cheapskatemonthly.com—Official Web site for *Cheapskate Monthly*

www.nodebtnews.com—Official Web site for No Debt Living.

FAST TRACK

1. A budget is simply a monthly spending plan. Your plan must include all of your expenses. It is not a good idea to "round" your figures. To be sure that you are working with exact

numbers, use your checkbook ledger or a printout from your financial software to get the job done.

2. A budget must include more than just your "bills," but also items such as haircuts, vehicle repairs, and other items that you don't receive a regular monthly bill for.

3. The key to financial success is spending less than you earn each month. Your extra money (financial surplus) will then be directed toward investing and debt reduction.

4. How you conduct your finances over the course of one month is likely to be a mirror image of your long-term financial habits.

5. Living on a budget can be fun. You many not believe it, but you can do a lot more for a lot less. If you pinch your pennies, they really will give you more than what you are getting now.

6. Being on a budget does not mean that you are the only one who will "cut back." You can learn how to cut the money you are paying to your banker, stockbroker, insurance agent, credit card company, and mortgage lender.

7. Of course, the reality is that life is a trade off. You will have to make choices; no financial strategy will allow you to spend unlimited amounts of money.

8. No two budgets are alike. It really does not matter the amount you spend on each category of expense as long as you are living within your means. Hey, if you want to spend all your money on clothing and live on cheese sandwiches, that is up to you.

9. If you are married, your budget should be a "family project." Successfully following a budget requires everyone's cooperation.

DAY 2 DIARY

I am on my way to my financial breakthrough. Today I . . .

_____

_____

_____

_____

_____

_____

_____

_____

_____

_____

_____

_____

_____

_____

_____

_____

_____

_____

_____

Day 3

Defeat Your Debt

S	M	T	W	T	F	S
	1	2	③	4	5	6

✔ This is the third day of your financial breakthrough. Today your focus is to determine how much debt you have, get a grasp on how much it is costing you, and most importantly create your own personal plan to become debt-free.

WHAT YOU WILL NEED:

- The current balances of all loan accounts (this includes any form of indebtedness: lines of credit, consolidation loans, credit cards, mortgages, etc.).
- The rate of interest you are paying on each of your debts.

CHRISTIAN MONEY PRINCIPLE

The Bible offers repeated warnings about debt. According to Proverbs 22:7, *"The rich rules over the poor, and the borrower is the*

slave of the lender" (RSV). It is clear from Scripture, and from evidence all around us, that debt can cause financial bondage. However, it is almost impossible to function in today's economy without incurring some form of debt. The caution is to use debt *wisely*.

Cashing In

Imagine you have $15,000 in credit card debt, with 18 percent interest. That will cost you $2,700 a year in interest alone! That $2,700 invested for 15 years at 11 percent would be worth $93,000. Which would you rather have: $93,000 in the bank, or the cancelled checks from having made $93,000 in credit card payments?

IS DEBT REALLY THAT BAD?

The answer to the question can vary greatly depending on whom you ask. In the Christian community, many financial and seminar teachers simply state that being in debt is wrong and people should not have debt for any reason. This again brings us to a dilemma of attempting to apply impractical advice to our daily lives. I believe that, in general, debt is overused in America and most people have a great deal of progress to make in this area of their personal finances. I am also convinced, however, that borrowing money *wisely* (the key word is wisely) can be a very positive part of building your net worth.

Questions to consider:

1. Are you borrowing money to live a lifestyle you cannot support?
2. Do you currently have a budget and financial management system in place that keeps you from spending more than you have coming in?

3. Do you know how much total debt you have and what it is costing you?
4. Have you formulated a plan to pay off your debts as a part of your plan to be financially independent?

There are many perspectives on how to borrow money wisely. Most of this advice is simple common sense, but let's cover the basics since they can never be emphasized enough.

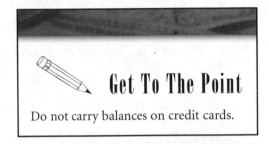

Get To The Point

Do not carry balances on credit cards.

CREDIT CARDS

Credit cards are a huge problem for many people because they provide easily accessible credit at very high interest rates. They are as close at hand as a wallet or purse and require nothing more than a quick swipe and a John Hancock; then the buyer is on his way.

This is a far different process than financing the purchase of a home. The buyer must first qualify for the loan, which involves mounds of paperwork. Then there are weeks of going back and forth with the mortgage lender, verifying income and credit history. Then the down payment—which can range from 3 percent to 20 percent of the purchase price—has to be paid with available cash. Finally, there is the closing where the buyer must physically appear at a title company to sign at least a dozen contracts to finalize everything. This is a process much more involved than reaching for a credit card and making an impulse purchase. I am not suggesting that everyone borrows wisely when purchasing a home, but credit card borrowing is definitely a more convenient and deceptive pitfall.

Much of the problem with establishing and following a budget is finding a way to account for credit card use. Often credit card purchases are "off budget" items. This means that the money being spent is not referenced anywhere. An easy solution to this is to obtain a debit card and use it as a check. With this system in place you would enter each credit card transaction in your checkbook just as if you had written a check. Many banks offer debit cards to their checking customers for a very small service charge. An alternative solution is to obtain a debit card that is completely separate from your checking account. Under this approach you would simply deposit a certain amount of money (that *is* budgeted for) on the card each month and then work off of that amount until it is gone.

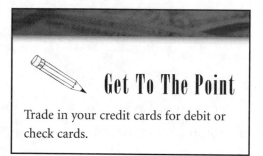

Get To The Point

Trade in your credit cards for debit or check cards.

I personally use a debit card like this for business travel. For accounting purposes I wanted to have a method of keeping all of my business travel expenses completely separate from my personal credit card accounts. Prior to each of my business trips my accountant makes a deposit to the business debit card account. All expenses for each trip are completely accounted for, and life is simple. Most importantly, I don't end up running a balance or paying high interest charges since everything is paid in advance. The only major drawback with debit cards is that many of them do not carry the same protection you may need in case of a transaction dispute. Be sure to read your cardholder agreement carefully to determine if you have the protection you need.

Another bonus that debit cards provide is that they can be obtained even with a bad credit record. Using a debit card responsibly is one method of rebuilding a poor credit file.

RECOMMENDED DEBIT (OR SECURED) CREDIT CARDS

(Look for secured credit card lists on www.tenday.com)

Amalgamated Bank of Chicago	(800) 723-0303
American Pacific Bank	(800) 610-1201
Banco Popular (Spanish)	(888) 642-2626
Bank One	(800) 544-4110
Chase Manhattan Bank USA	(800) 482-4223
Citibank	(800) 743-1332
Cross Country Bank	(561) 982-9111
First Consumers National Bank	(800) 876-3262
First National Bank of Brookings	(800) 658-3660
First Premier Bank	(800) 987-5521
People's Bank	(800) 426-1114
Sterling Bank & Trust	(800) 767-0923
Union Planters Bank	(800) 362-6299
Union Plus/Household Bank	(800) 622-2580
United Bank of Philadelphia	(800) 255-3807
United California Bank	(866) 226-5822
Washington Mutual	(800) 884-1789
Wells Fargo Card Services	(800) 642-4720

DEBT BREAKTHROUGH WORKSHEET

Name of Creditor	Interest Rate	Amount Owed

Your Total Debt _____

MAKING THE TURN

The critical task you need to accomplish today is to develop a plan to reduce your credit card debt as quickly as possible. If you follow a practical and reasonable plan, your debt will decline each month and it will soon disappear altogether. After evaluating how much credit card debt you have, and realizing how much you're paying in interest charges on these balances, the picture will come into focus very clearly. If you have minimal debt, you are in the minority. If not, this section will be one of the most important for your financial breakthrough.

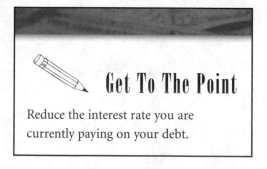

Get To The Point

Reduce the interest rate you are currently paying on your debt.

During day two we discussed the importance of creating a surplus so that you can make a monthly payment toward financial freedom. The key

54

to quickly paying off a debt is to pay as much as possible each month on the principal balance. One obvious way to do that is to make a higher payment each month, but a second method that does not require increasing your payment at all is to reduce your interest rate. When you combine both a reduction of interest rate with an increase in your monthly payment, your debt will disappear faster than you ever imagined.

According to the Bankcard Holders of America, if you make the minimum payment required (and don't make any additional purchases) it will take about twenty-five years to pay off the balance! This is because the average credit card interest rate is almost 18 percent, and since most "minimum payments" are applied almost entirely to interest, very little is applied to the principal. Credit card companies have laid the groundwork to keep you perpetually in debt. I have learned that a simple move from a high interest credit card to a lower rate alternative will cut years off your payments.

CONSIDER THE FOLLOWING EXAMPLE

Big Balance Betty has a $10,000 balance on a credit card with an 18 percent interest rate. If she paid the minimum monthly payment of $152, she would be in debt for twenty-four years.

If Betty transferred this balance to a 10 percent credit card and made the same payment each month, she would be out of debt in eight years, saving an amazing sixteen years of payments. Even better, if Betty were to get a home equity loan, she could pay off this credit card, make the same $152 monthly payments to the lender for seven years (not eight), *and* get a tax deduction on the interest she paid. (Go Betty! Go Betty!)

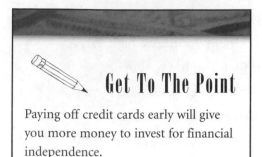

Get To The Point

Paying off credit cards early will give you more money to invest for financial independence.

WHAT THIS CAN DO FOR YOUR FINANCIAL FUTURE

As you can see from Betty's example, switching to a low interest rate credit card can save sixteen years worth of $152 monthly payments. So what? Can that really make a difference in *your* life? Well, let's see. . . . What if you redirected that $152 into a mutual fund for sixteen years and averaged an 11 percent return per year? What might happen? You would accumulate $79,000! I don't know about you, but accumulating a lump sum of $79,000 in my financial independence account is far more appealing than writing checks to pay interest to a credit card company for sixteen years. Pause for a moment and consider the fact that this is just *one* simple change you can make in your financial life—and a huge benefit is gained. This does not even require that you increase what you are paying each month, just lower your interest rate!

WHAT SHOULD YOU DO FIRST?

You now realize that you have allowed those credit cards to get out of control, and you are facing several balances to pay on two or more cards. What do you do? This is a question I've received many times throughout the years, so I can only assume that it is a fairly widespread problem. The first thing you should do when you realize you have this problem is *stay calm*. Don't allow yourself to panic or to become overwhelmed by the bills that seem to be surrounding you now. The best thing to do is to lay out each of the bills in front of you and formulate a systematic plan for paying them off. It is not as difficult a task as it may appear, and the key to being successful is to be patient and diligent and stick to your plan. There are basically two paths you can take when implementing this systematic type of plan, and I've found that each can be quite successful in its own right.

The first method is known as the "highest rate" plan. This means that you organize your bills in a way that allows you to concentrate on paying down the one with the highest interest rate first, the next highest interest rate second, and so on. To implement this plan most effectively, you should work up a monthly budget for yourself. The goal here is to try to determine how much

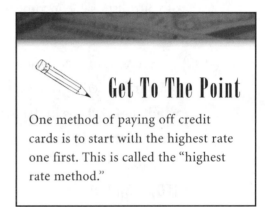

Get To The Point

One method of paying off credit cards is to start with the highest rate one first. This is called the "highest rate method."

disposable income (or "extra money") you have at the end of each month after you make the minimum monthly payments on all of your credit cards and bills. A good rule of thumb is to divide the amount of your disposable income by three, then take one of those thirds and send it to the high-rate credit card issuer (this is, of course, in addition to the minimum payment which you're already sending them). Once you have completely paid down that card, move on to the next-highest card and repeat the process. With the remaining two-thirds of your disposable income, you can pay down other debt—or invest. But don't let that money just disappear.

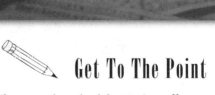

Get To The Point

The second method for paying off credit card debt is to start with the account having the lowest balance. This is called the "lowest balance method."

The second method is known as the "lowest balance method." With the "lowest balance" plan you concentrate on paying off the card with the lowest total balance, without regard to the interest rate. The benefit to this is that you can more quickly eliminate one of your card balances, which gives you a feeling of accomplishment. You would apply a portion of your disposable income to the card with the lowest balance in the same way you would toward the card with the highest interest rate.

I have found both of these methods to be excellent, but you must remain focused. If you happen to receive some type of unexpected windfall—perhaps in the form of a tax refund—play it smart: Apply as much of that windfall as you can toward the credit card you are paying off.

AUTOMOBILE DEBT

Most of us have at least one vehicle—many have two. The question is: What kind of vehicle do we really need? Despite pressure from auto dealers to buy the latest and greatest powerful, sporty, or luxurious car, what most of us need is a reliable vehicle to take us from point A to point B. The best approach to buying a vehicle is to purchase a slightly-used car and finance it for two years—instead of five years as most banks and loaning institutions suggest. If you simply cannot handle the payments of a 2-year loan, consider owning fewer cars or, at the very least, make additional payments on your loan (and make sure they are applied to principal).

HOME MORTGAGE DEBT

Although some would discourage home ownership if it requires going into debt, I believe that this can be one of the most justifiable reasons to borrow money.

Borrowing money to buy a home is different than accumulating credit card debt. Here's why:

- Over time, real estate is an appreciating asset.
- Interest paid on a home mortgage is tax deductible.
- The interest rate for mortgages is significantly less than a typical credit card or other forms of consumer debt.

The reality is that we all must have a place to live. Unless you are living rent-free or do not plan to stay in one place for more than three to four years, you should consider the benefits of buying a home.

The most important decision you will face when buying a home is the type of mortgage you will use to finance your purchase. If you do not carefully select the right mortgage for your situation, the results may well affect whether or not you can enjoy your purchase. In extreme cases, the

Get To The Point

If you buy a home, choose the best mortgage for your circumstances.

wrong mortgage can even cause you to lose your home, so you need to pay careful attention to the terms in the contract.

There are two basic types of mortgages: fixed and variable. A fixed mortgage has an interest rate and monthly payment that stays the same throughout the life of the mortgage. With a variable mortgage, the rate you pay can (and probably will) change during the term of the mortgage as interest rates fluctuate. Fixed mortgages are the most popular because they give peace of mind to the buyers, who know that the rate they settle on at the beginning of the mortgage will never change. Adjustable-rate mortgage costs will move in the same direction as interest rates, which means that your payments could go either up or down during the term of the mortgage. There are some good reasons to choose an adjustable-rate mortgage, but the uncertainty that comes with them makes them less popular overall.

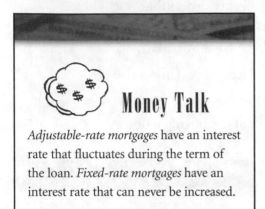

Money Talk

Adjustable-rate mortgages have an interest rate that fluctuates during the term of the loan. *Fixed-rate mortgages* have an interest rate that can never be increased.

Lenders often use adjustable-rate mortgages to entice prospective homebuyers into giving their loan business to them. They do this by offering the loan at an artificially low rate for the first year or two, with the understanding that the rate will increase as interest rates go up. For example, if the average rate for a fixed mortgage is 8.25 percent, it's likely that you would be able to secure an adjustable-rate mortgage that requires you to pay about 7 percent for the first year or two of ownership.

Some homebuyers are seduced by the lower-rate adjustable loans and get into a house that is out of their price range. That can be dangerous. When rates move upward, the home owners eventually find themselves with a monthly payment they can't afford.

Under specific circumstances, an adjustable-rate mortgage can be a good choice. If, for example, you decide to purchase a home even though you believe you'll only be there for a few years, the adjustable rate would likely be the way to go. Then you can pay the artificially low rate, and when the payments begin to increase, you'll be ready to move. Also, if you opt for an adjustable mortgage at a time when interest rates are headed downward, your rate will decrease as well. Keep in mind that if you happen to have a fixed mortgage, when rates go down you can refinance the contract on your house at the new lower rate. Generally, though, adjustable rate mortgages are not the best approach.

Spend your efforts trying to secure the lowest fixed-rate mortgage you can find. Fixed-rate mortgages come in two different types or lengths: thirty-year and fifteen-year. Most homeowners have the standard thirty-year mortgage chiefly because

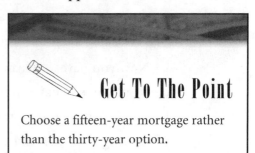

Get To The Point

Choose a fifteen-year mortgage rather than the thirty-year option.

the payments are lower. Don't make the mistake, however, of thinking that a fifteen-year mortgage costs twice as much as a thirty-year mortgage with the same interest rate. The payments on a fifteen-year loan will be higher, but they are not twice as high. That's because of the way that the time value of money works. Let's look at a quick example.

Suppose you want to purchase a $100,000 home. If you are able to qualify for a thirty-year mortgage at 9 percent interest, your monthly payments will be $805. A fifteen-year mortgage at the same 9 percent interest rate will cost $1,015 per month. It's true that $1,015 is higher than $805, but it's only about $200 more, not another $805 more. If you can afford to pay the higher figure, then you'll save thousands of dollars in interest and own your home a lot sooner.

During a season of falling interest rates, it makes sense to seriously consider the possibility of refinancing. One rule of thumb says to refinance if you can save 1.5 to 2 percent on your current loan, but like many of these "rules" it tends to oversimplify an important decision that deserves much more careful consideration. If you are considering refinancing your mortgage, start by obtaining several quotes to get an idea of what interest rates are currently available. Also ask what your new payment would be (including the costs of refinancing). The new payment should be significantly lower or it would make not sense to even consider the proposition of refinancing.

Now you have an idea if this is the right time to consider a new loan. But you still have an important step to take. You will need to determine how many payments it will take to recover the costs of refinancing. Consider this example: If the total costs of refinancing are $3,000, and you saved $100 per month with your "new payment," it would take thirty months to break even. It would take thirty months ($3,000 divided by the $100 monthly savings), or two and a half years, to reach the point where your new loan will result in saving you money every month. Of course, one important factor that makes refinancing much easier is the many offers of low-cost and no-cost refinance deals that are now available. Although the mortgage lender may agree to dramatically cut their charges, you will still have significant other expenses when refinancing. These costs include various governmental fees (depending on where you live), title insurance, and numerous other charges.

One way that I have saved hundreds of dollars when refinancing over the years is to request the "reissue rate" on my title insurance. This is much less expensive than purchasing a new policy and can make a significant difference in your overall closing costs. I personally saved $800 when I asked for the reissue rate. The person I was dealing with seemed surprised I had heard of it. (It feels so good to be "in the know!")

Money Talk

A *reissued* insurance policy is an update of an existing policy, without the commission fees.

Prior to closing, most states require that you receive a "Good Faith Estimate" of what the closing costs will be. Once you receive this itemized breakdown, it is your final chance to take the deal or walk away. In any case, regardless of what the total costs are to refinance, do the simple calculation, and you will readily know whether it makes sense to pursue it or not.

One last thought on the decision to refinance: Be careful to understand where you are in your amortization schedule. If you started with a thirty-year mortgage and are now in year twenty or greater, you may not be paying very much interest in each payment. This is because long-term mortgage loans charge most of the interest in the first half of the loan. Consequently, most of the payment in later years is principal. If you have reached the point in your loan where you are not paying much interest, refinancing will not be of much value to you. Order a copy of your amortization schedule from your current lender to make a final determination.

Of course, refinancing is only part of the solution. Without following a consistent payment plan and taking advantage of early pay-off opportunities, you will miss out on your greatest opportunity to eliminate your debt and protect your investment. Do you have difficulty remembering to make your mortgage payment on time? Consider a bi-weekly mortgage plan if you want to go on "auto pilot." These popular plans are based on making a mortgage payment every two weeks instead of once per month. These plans actually will cut ten years or more off of a traditional thirty-year mortgage.

If you make a payment every two weeks, you will make twenty-six half payments every year. This is the equivalent of making thirteen full payments. The "extra payment" occurs because some months have five weeks, and over the course of a year this adds up to an additional payment (based on the "every two week approach"). The companies offering these services do have service charges and other expenses that they pass along. As such, it is easier and less expensive to just make one extra full payment each year and you will duplicate the results of the bi-weekly plan for free. The bi-weekly plans are good, however, if you are not disciplined enough to do it on your own.

 ## INTERNET TIME SAVERS

www.christianmoney.com—Subscribers to my Christian Money Net service have access to my confidential low-interest rate credit card list.

www.money.com—*Money Magazine* provides lists of not only the best credit card rates, but also information on auto loans and home mortgage rates as well.

www.myratesaver.com—My number one recommendation. They work with all kinds of refinancing and can even help if you have bad credit.

www.eloan.com—Allows you to do a nationwide search for loans of all types.

www.lendingtree.com—Allows you to do a nationwide search for loans of all types.

www.smartmoney.com—Offers a unique debt calculator service that will help you determine the real cost of your debt.

www.bankrate.com—Provides lists of low-interest rate credit card options and other resources like secured credit card services.

www.quicken.com—Provides a debt-reduction calculator service.

www.tenday.com—Offers a debt-reduction planner service.

www.hsh.com—Offers a series of mortgage calculator services.

FAST TRACK

1. Much of the problem with establishing and following a budget is finding a way to account for credit card use. An easy solution to this is to obtain a debit card and use it as a check.

2. When you combine a reduction of interest rate with an increase in your monthly payment, your debt will disappear faster than you ever imagined.

3. A simple move from a high interest credit card to a lower rate alternative will cut years off your payments.

4. The best approach to buying a vehicle is to purchase a slightly-used car and finance it for two years—instead of five years as most banks and loaning institutions suggest.

5. Always opt for a fifteen-year mortgage rather than a thirty-year mortgage. If you already have a thirty-year mortgage, add about 20 percent extra to each payment, and you will pay it off in fifteen.

6. Make extra principal payments on your mortgage as frequently as possible. Obtain a copy of your amortization schedule for your lender, and you will see that it may take only an extra $75 to $100 to wipe out the equivalent of an entire future payment of $1,000 or more!

7. Using a bi-weekly mortgage payment plan can cut ten years or more off of a traditional thirty-year mortgage.

DAY 3 DIARY

I am on my way to my financial breakthrough. Today I . . .

_____

_____

_____

_____

_____

_____

_____

_____

_____

_____

_____

_____

_____

_____

_____

_____

_____

Day 4

Tackle Your Taxes

S	M	T	W	T	F	S
	1	2	3	④	5	6

✔ Today you are going to tackle the dreaded subject that makes even the bravest souls run for cover: taxes! Today you will determine your marginal tax rate, learn how to cut your taxes, understand the value of finding a tax deduction, and discover how to find deductions and tax credits that you can use to substantially cut your tax bill. All of this will lead to more money in your pocket and less eaten up by taxes.

WHAT YOU WILL NEED:

- Copies of your most recent tax returns (last three years, if available).
- Most recent pay stubs from your employer(s).
- Your checkbook ledger (or, if available, a printout of your checking transactions for the past year from a financial software program).

- The ability to go on-line to the IRS Web site www.irs.gov to read the fine print and restrictions on the strategies covered in this chapter.

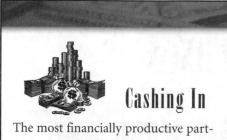

Cashing In

The most financially productive part-time job available could be working on reducing your taxes. It is estimated that we all work each year until the month of May just to pay our tax bill. How much can you save? It will vary based on your income and how tax savvy you already are. Don't be surprised if you are able to find hundreds of dollars or more in lost tax deductions. What if you could save just $300 per year on taxes? If you invested this money for 25 years at an 11 percent return it would grow to $34,000!

Taxes are usually accepted as just another expenditure we are stuck with. Tax planning is generally viewed as something only for the rich. And looking for deductions is sometimes seen as a dishonest search for methods of getting around the law. There is absolutely no moral problem or shortcoming in taking full advantage of every legal tax deduction you are entitled to. I cannot even begin to count the number of times married couples have informed me that the reason they both have to work is because of taxes.

In many cases, an amount equal to one spouse's entire salary goes to pay the family's tax liability. I will not use this chapter as a platform to engage in a debate about the fairness of the U.S. tax system. I think it is objective to write that most Americans believe that the current system is far too complicated, requires that we pay too much of our income into it, and in the end seems to have an insatiable desire for more and more of our money. I will not attempt to make you an expert on tax law today, but I will give you the 90 percent that you can use to make an immediate improvement in your tax picture. When I write immediate, I mean that literally. In fact, you may be able to increase the amount of your very next paycheck by a hefty sum after following the advice in this chapter.

WHAT TAXES DO YOU PAY?

You may find it startling when you sit down and consider the myriad ways you are taxed. Just as an exercise, you may want to sit down and make a list of all of the other taxes that you regularly pay.

- Real estate tax
- Sales tax
- Gas tax
- Utility tax

This does not even factor in the reality that every product or service you buy from a corporation has some level of taxes already "built in" to the price. This is because corporations are also subject to all of these taxes and simply pass that expense on to you the consumer.

HOW IS MY TAX LIABILITY DETERMINED?

The U.S. tax code provides individuals two choices when filing a tax return. You can itemize, which involves adding up all of your tax deductions and using them to offset your income, or select the "standard deduction." This means that you don't have many deductions and are instead taking the government's base amount. Selecting the standard deduction is easier, but it will mean that you are going to pay the

Money Talk

Your tax liability is the amount of taxes you owe.

maximum amount in taxes dollar for dollar on your level of income. The IRS estimates that about one-third of taxpayers select the standard deduction rather than itemizing. Not everyone can itemize. Some people simply do not have enough deductions to make the choice to itemize. If you fall into that category, read on. I have some suggestions on how you can increase your deductions (and keep more of your money).

Money Talk

The standard deduction is a flat amount you can take rather than listing your tax deductible expenses on your return.

The amount of the standard deduction for the year 2000 was as follows:

Married filing jointly:	$7,350
Married filing separately:	$3,675
Single:	$4,400
Head of household:	$6,450

Whether you itemize or choose the standard deduction, you are also eligible to deduct a fixed amount for each dependent (including yourself). The personal exemption amount for the year 2000 was $2,800 per person. The matter of who you can claim as a dependent can be tricky. I have read stories of individuals claiming pets as dependents and other strange applications of this tax code section. While this shows a certain amount of creativity, Fido and Fluffy are not legal dependents and, thus, cannot be claimed as such on your tax return. A dependent, according to the IRS, is any person to whom you are providing at least 50 percent or more of their financial support (based on meeting other requirements). There are, of course, complicated circumstances such as an adult child who contributes to the finances of their elderly parents. In this example, it is possible that supporting a parent could qualify for the dependent exemption, but several other requirements must be met. Only one person can claim the dependent, so be sure get specific information from the IRS Web site or discuss this matter with your tax advisor to avoid any confusion.

WHAT PERCENTAGE OF MY INCOME DO I PAY IN TAXES?

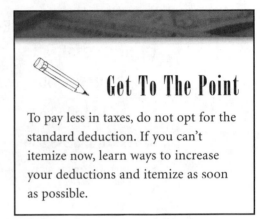

Get To The Point

To pay less in taxes, do not opt for the standard deduction. If you can't itemize now, learn ways to increase your deductions and itemize as soon as possible.

Depending on your filing status, your income after adjustments (such as contributions to an IRA or some other tax deductible retirement account), deductions, tax credits, and personal exemptions, are applied to a sliding scale that determines how much tax you owe. These schedules are commonly called the "Tax Tables."

2000 TAX RATES ON INCOME—MARRIED FILING JOINTLY

Up to $43,850	15 %
$43,851 to $105,950	28 %
$105,951 to $161,450	31 %
$161,451 to $288,350	36 %
More than $288,350	39.6 %

2000 TAX RATES ON INCOME—MARRIED FILING SEPARATELY

Up to $21,925	15 %
$21,926 to $52,975	28 %

$52,976 to $80,725	31 %
$80,726 to $144,175	36 %
More than $144,175	39.6 %

2000 TAX RATES ON INCOME—SINGLE

Up to $26,250	15 %
$26,251 to $63,550	28 %
$$63,551 to $132,600	31 %
$132,601 to $288,350	36 %
More than $288,350	39.6 %

2000 TAX RATES ON INCOME—HEAD OF HOUSEHOLD

Up to $35,150	15 %
$35,151 to $90,800	28 %
$90,801 to $147,050	31 %
$147,051 to $288,350	36 %
More than $288,350	39.6 %

Why do some married couples file separate tax returns? The most common reason is to avoid joint liability. If you file a tax return with your spouse, you can be held liable for his or her taxes. Because of this risk, you may not want to file jointly. Many business owners do not want their spouses to be exposed to the liability that could stem from an IRS audit of their business or even the possibility that the business may fail and not have enough money to pay its final tax bill.

WHAT IS A "TAX BRACKET"?

A person earning less than $35,150 a year (after applying that income to one of the IRS tax tables) may look at the tax rates and think, "OK, I have to pay 15 percent of that to the government." Good answer. Now ask that same person how much they pay if they get a raise and earn $45,000 (nice raise, eh?). Most people are tempted to say they would now have to pay 28 percent of that $45,000. That is not the case. Actually, that person would pay 15 percent on the first $35,150. The difference (roughly $10,000 in this case) is what is taxed at the 28 percent rate. This person's *marginal tax rate* is 28 percent. This is because the term *marginal tax rate* is defined as the highest percentage on the tax tables that your income reaches. Even though this person pays most of his or her taxes at the 15 percent rate, they are considered to be at the 28 percent marginal tax rate. This person's *effective tax rate* is the actual percentage of taxable income that gets paid in taxes overall. Make sense? Not really? Read on.

The amount that you pay as an overall percentage of your income is your *effective tax rate*. For example, a married couple filing a joint return has taxable income of $105,000. These taxpayers would be in the 28

Money Talk

Married couples will usually pay more than singles. This has been called the *marriage penalty*. The new tax law has substantially reduced this penalty for most married people, but not eliminated it.

Money Talk

Your *effective tax rate* is the actual percentage of your taxable income that you pay in taxes.

percent marginal tax bracket. This means that the highest rate (highest level their income was assessed on the tax table) is 28 percent. This is the percentage that they paid on their *last dollar of income* (the amount which causes them to be bumped into the next higher bracket). The amount owed in taxes overall would be $23,700 or about 23 percent (effective tax rate). So while they are in the 28 percent bracket, they are effectively only paying 23 percent of their taxable income in taxes (after adjustments, deductions, and exemptions).

Get To The Point

Your tax bracket is the rate you pay on the last dollar of your income.

CAPITAL GAINS TAXES

Federal taxes are paid not only on the income you make at work. Taxes are also paid on the profit made from the sale of a capital asset. Capital assets are usually either real estate or securities (investments like mutual funds, stocks, and bonds). If you lose money on the sale of an asset, you receive a tax deduction. You can offset capital losses with capital gains. You can also use up to $3,000 of capital losses per year to offset income. Other than this $3,000 limit, you must use capital losses to offset capital gains. The good news is that you can carry forward your capital losses until you are able to completely use them, even if it takes several years to do so.

Assets held for one year or longer are taxed at a maximum rate of 20 percent (long-term capital gains rate). Taxpayers in the lowest income tax rate of 15 percent only pay 10 percent on long-term capital gains (subject to certain maximums). Assets held less than one year are subject to a maximum capital gains rate of 28 percent (short-term capital gains). Again, individuals in lower income tax brackets may be eligible for lower rates. Real estate profits may also enjoy a lower maximum tax rate of just 25 percent in many cases.

What all of this means is that if you buy a stock or a mutual fund and it goes up in value, Uncle Sam wants his share of the profit. There are ways to avoid this tax which we will discuss during day five. In a nutshell, by utilizing tax-preferenced accounts like IRAs, mutual fund annuities, or company retirement plans, you can defer these taxes for decades. In the case of a Roth IRA, the money you withdraw during retirement is never taxed! The important lesson to learn here is that you must not only be focused on making money with your investments, but avoiding taxes on your profits and, at a minimum, delaying the taxes for as long as possible.

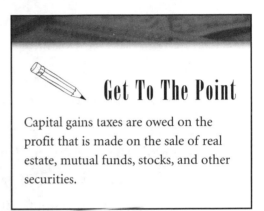

Get To The Point

Capital gains taxes are owed on the profit that is made on the sale of real estate, mutual funds, stocks, and other securities.

WHAT IS THE REAL VALUE OF A TAX DEDUCTION?

People with legitimate and necessary expenses for their business can benefit by getting them at a "discount" after applying the tax deduction. No arguments there. Smart business owners can, and should, take advantage of every legal tax deduction. This idea, however, is only good to a point. I have observed individuals foolishly spending money on questionable purchases only to justify them because of the tax deduction. Let's examine the "logic" of this more closely.

Self-employed Sam decides to purchase cellular phone service because he heard it was a "good tax deduction." While he really does not need the phone (he has another cell phone for personal use), and it will not increase his business potential, he signs up because of the deduction. Sam spends $750 a year for the service. It is a legitimate tax deduction because the phone is used exclusively for his business. Sam is in the 28 percent marginal tax bracket, so he would save 28 percent of the $750 (.28 x $750), or about $210. The actual amount of money saved is $540 less than what was spent to purchase the service. As you can see, the tax deduction alone does not justify the purchase. In reality, Sam just spent $540 to buy a $210 tax benefit. Not a real smart one, Sam.

It is a myth that extravagant purchases are OK if they can be claimed as a deduction. Another myth is promoted by some authors who write books that claim you can all but wipe out your tax liability completely. This is just not reality. The most you can hope to do is to substantially reduce your tax liability by creating a smart tax plan.

TAX DEDUCTION REMINDERS

- If you are an employee, you cannot take any deduction for unreimbursed employee expenses unless they exceed 2 percent (known as the 2 percent floor).
- Only medical expenses that exceed 7.5 percent of your adjusted gross income are tax deductible.
- If you are self-employed in your own business (filing schedule C), your qualifying business expenses would not be subject to any "floor," but are deductible from the first dollar.

VALUABLE TAX DEDUCTIONS

REAL ESTATE

Purchase a home rather than renting. (Interest on a home mortgage loan is tax deductible while rent payments on a residence are not.) Another deduction-rich opportunity is to purchase rental property. As an owner of rental property, you are eligible to take an annual depreciation allowance. The amount is based on a 27-year schedule. The amount of your depreciation deduction can be thousands of dollars per year (based on the purchase price of the real estate). Rental real estate is also a tremendous way to build wealth for the future. It is very common to find that 80 percent or more of a person's net worth at retirement is home equity. Why not own an additional home as a rental property and have twice the real estate to cash in at your retirement (not to mention the valuable tax deductions)? As an owner of rental real estate, you are also eligible for other deductions such as advertising, maintenance, and property management fees, just to name a few.

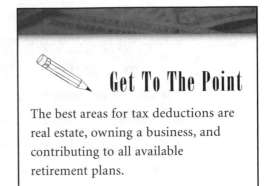

Get To The Point

The best areas for tax deductions are real estate, owning a business, and contributing to all available retirement plans.

BUSINESS EXPENSES

The government helps encourage entrepreneurial pursuits by offering generous tax deductions. The day you go into business, you become eligible for dozens of tax deductions that you

Get To The Point

Owning a business means significant tax deductions.

would otherwise not have access to. Find something you would enjoy doing which can be done profitably.

As mentioned previously, it does not make financial sense to set up a small business and go out and foolishly spend money just for the tax deductions. The idea is to combine a great business concept with the added benefit of a host of newly found tax deductions. The key to a legitimate tax deduction—as opposed to tax fraud—is that you are genuinely expending money in the attempt to make money in your business. Some books teach that you can go on a vacation and make one stop for business along the way and write off the whole trip. This sounds good, but is not legal. To the extent that you use your car, computer, VCR, a home office, and other business-related items, they may provide tax deductions to you on Schedule C of your tax return. To learn more about the myriad of new tax deductions you will be eligible for, call the Internal Revenue Service at (800) 829-1049 and request publication #334. According to the IRS, you become eligible for these business deductions "the day you have an intent to make a profit." Consequently, you don't even have to wait until you order your business cards to start keeping a file of your expenses.

Rather than go into extreme detail on all of the potential tax deductions available, I will refer you to IRS publication #334. Two deductions that are worth mentioning here are the home-office deduction and business travel. Depending on the type of small business you start, you may be able to travel on business and write off your trips. You must follow the IRS guidelines, but there are numerous ways of combining business with pleasure and getting a tax deduction for your travel. You could attend a seminar at an exotic location or schedule your trip around a weekend. Conduct business on Friday and Monday and sightsee in between. I have seen some of the most beautiful places during my business travel.

Because I am a sports fanatic, one of the first things I do when my plane lands in a new city is find out if there are any sporting events taking place while I am in town. If there are none, my second choice is to see a live theater production. While the cost of my tickets to these events is not tax deductible (unless I take a client as a guest), the amount of my travel to get to that city and my lodging are. Do be careful, though, as the IRS has very strict rules regarding business travel expenses. Be sure you understand them carefully before proceeding. Also be aware that your business must become profitable within about three years or it could be deemed a "hobby" and you would not be eligible to take any further related deductions.

RETIREMENT PLANS

One of the most overlooked methods of saving money on taxes is to simply take advantage of your company's qualified retirement plan. If you own a business you can start a small business retirement plan. Based on the new tax law, you may be able to shelter up to $40,000. Money contributed to your company retirement plan is not included in your income and grows inside your retirement plan without being taxed until you withdraw it. The new tax law also provides a tax credit of up to $1,000 (depending on your income) for making as little as a $2,000 contribution to a qualified retirement plan. Consult with a professional tax adviser to learn if these new laws may apply to you. You may also wish to consider other tax shelter opportunities such as mutual fund annuities. While they don't provide a tax deduction, the money invested is not taxed until it is withdrawn from the account.

TAX CREDITS

A tax credit is not the same as a tax deduction. It's better. In the world of tax savings, it is the crown jewel. A tax credit is a dollar-for-

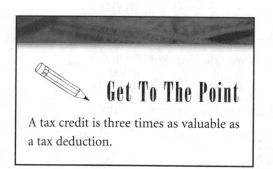

Get To The Point

A tax credit is three times as valuable as a tax deduction.

dollar reduction in your taxes. If you owed $1,000 to the IRS, but have a $1,000 tax credit, you would owe nothing. Unlike the earlier example in this chapter which shows a tax deduction is only worth a percentage of each dollar spent, the tax credit is more than three times as powerful as most tax deductions.

MAJOR TAX CREDIT PROGRAMS

Dependent Child Credit—$500 per child under age seventeen and incrementally increasing to $800 by 2009.

Adoption Expense Credit—Based on your income, you may be eligible for up to a $6,000 tax credit to offset expenses incurred in the adoption of a child.

Dependent Care Credit—If you incur expenses for child care so that you can work, you may be eligible for a tax credit of up to 20 percent of those expenses.

Earned Income Credit—This credit can be worth more than $3,000. The credit is for lower income individuals with children living at home.

(Note: The tax credit information above is based on the laws in effect for the year 2000. Before claiming these credits on your income tax returns, be sure you have up-to-date information for the current tax year.)

Get To The Point

The new tax law passed in 2001 may provide your family with even greater opportunities for tax savings.

AN OVERVIEW OF THE NEW TAX LAW

- New tax rates will be gradually phased in through the year 2006. Marginal tax rates will come down 3 percent in each bracket (except the 15 percent bracket), and there will be an introduction of a new 10 percent marginal rate.
- Dependent care expense deductions will increase to a maximum of $3,000 (from a current maximum of $2,400).
- By 2005, the marriage penalty will be substantially reduced.
- Amounts you can contribute to your IRA will increase.
- Contribution limits on what you can contribute to 401k and other company-sponsored retirement plans will increase substantially.
- Tax credit will be given for contributing to retirement plans. Depending on your income you may be able to get a tax credit for up to 50 percent of your first $2,000 contributed. For example, a married couple could get a $1,000 tax credit for making a contribution of $2,000 to an IRA. This is above and beyond the tax benefits of the IRA itself.
- Education expenses may be eligible for a variety of new tax benefits (too many to list here). Read your tax return instructions for information on how you may qualify for any or all of these tax benefits.

GETTING ORGANIZED

It is important that everyone learn to prepare his or her own tax return. This is not to save money spent on a tax preparer, as that is not a very expensive proposition these days. The purpose of doing your own taxes is to learn all of the potential tax deductions that you may be eligible for. Even the best tax preparer will not be able to follow you around for a year and learn your habits to ensure that you do not miss any tax deductions. The software program that I use is Turbo Tax. I love the program since it not only provides a computer-based means of preparing my tax return, but it also has a number of other interactive features that make missing a tax deduction almost impossible. One of the first steps in using Turbo Tax is to complete an interactive questionnaire that, when finished, provides you with a complete list of all of your "potential" deductions.

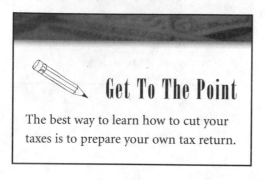

Get To The Point

The best way to learn how to cut your taxes is to prepare your own tax return.

GO ON A TAX DEDUCTION HUNT

A helpful tax tool is one of the major tax guides that are available at your local bookstore or library. I personally prefer the *J.K. Lasser Guide*. A simple exercise is to look through the table of contents and

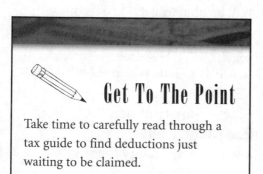

Get To The Point

Take time to carefully read through a tax guide to find deductions just waiting to be claimed.

place a check mark next to any item that involves a deduction you might be eligible for. A great way to do this is to use your checkbook register as you a search through the tax guide for each of your "possible deductions." These tax guides sell for about $20 and are worth every dollar if you use them to complete this simple exercise.

Here are some possible deductions you may be eligible for:

- One-time contributions to charities.
- Membership dues, trade magazine subscriptions, or uniform purchases necessary for your job that your employer does not pay for.
- Classes you take in order to get a promotion.

WHAT TO DO ABOUT THE PAST

Once you begin finding tax deductions that you qualify for, you may realize that you have missed the opportunity in years past to significantly lower your taxes. What can you do if the IRS kept too much of your money? If you have tax deductions or credits from past years that you did not take full credit for, you can easily go back and file an amended return. The IRS will allow you to go back as far as three years and resubmit a new tax return.

HOW TO INCREASE YOUR TAKE-HOME PAY NOW

You may remember the first day of employment at your current job, when you were required to complete a W-4 form. This form is used to determine the amount that is withheld from your paycheck each pay period. The idea behind withholding is that taxpayers are

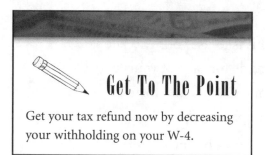

Get To The Point

Get your tax refund now by decreasing your withholding on your W-4.

required to pay at least 90 percent of their tax liability prior to the end of the tax year. Most people have too much money withheld which results in a refund in the spring. Although getting a tax refund may seem like an exciting proposition, it is not a good use of your money. The IRS holds on to your money for a year or longer and pays you no interest at all.

A better idea is to update your W-4 and begin taking home a large paycheck right now. This increased "take-home pay" can be used to fund a retirement account. Be careful not to go too far with this strategy because you will be subject to penalties if you are under-withheld for the year. Remember: You must pay the IRS at least 90 percent of what your tax liability will be for the year, or you may face penalties.

IRS AUDITS

Fewer than 2 percent of all tax returns are audited, but that does not mean that it will never happen. My policy is to take every tax deduction I am legally entitled to. I do not pass up any deduction because of the fear of being audited. There are a number of services that provide audit protection. The one I recommend is Pre-Paid Legal Services. For just $26 per month, you become eligible for a wide array of services, including unlimited access to attorneys by phone, preparation of your will, trial defense, and legal representation in the event of an audit. If you are interested in this type of service, please visit www.tenday.com for more information.

⏰ INTERNET TIME SAVERS

www.irs.gov—The official IRS Web site. The most useful part of this site is the search feature which provides an easy method to get information on any tax topic you are interested in. You can download tax forms and even apply for an extension to file on-line. If you are looking for a job, employment opportunities are posted on the site.

www.taxhelponline.com—This site is published by Daniel Pilla. If you owe money to the IRS and cannot pay in full, you should go to this site. Dan provides a series of easy methods for negotiating with the IRS, including how to get your tax bill reduced to pennies on the dollar.

www.irs.com—The official H & R Block Web site. Although they use "IRS" in their domain name, there is no affiliation. This is really a tremendous site with a huge amount of resources.

www.taxsites.com—This site does not provide any of its own resources, but provides links to just about every place on the web that offers tax assistance. This may be the only site you will need on the issue.

FAST TRACK

1. Your best part-time job could be working on reducing your taxes.
2. Determine what your marginal tax rate is. This will help you to know the value of any tax deductions you may uncover.
3. Try to itemize rather than selecting the standard deduction. This will usually result in a smaller tax bill.
4. The most tax-deduction-rich opportunities are retirement accounts (IRAs, 401ks, and other company plans), real estate

(both owning your own home and purchasing rental properties), and starting a business. Consider whether you can take advantage of any of these tax-saving opportunities.

5. Taxes paid on profit from the sale of stocks, real estate, and other capital assets are known as capital gains taxes. These tax rates range from 20-28 percent for most people. The amount of tax owed is based on how long you hold the investment before you sell. If you sell in less than one year you will be taxed at a higher short-term rate, while assets held for longer that one year are subject to a lower long-term rate. Consider avoiding capital gains taxes by making your investments inside an IRA, mutual fund annuity, or other tax shelter.

6. Consider purchasing Turbo Tax computer software and preparing you own tax return. This software package helps reduce the chances of missing deductions and credits and has the added benefit of making you more "tax savvy" if you personally get involved with your tax return. You can purchase Turbo Tax on-line at www.intuit.com.

7. If you expect to receive a significant tax refund in the spring it is better to decrease your withholding on form W-4, which you can request from your employer. Once you reduce your withholding, you will automatically increase your "take-home pay."

8. Go on a tax deduction hunt. You will need a tax guide and your checkbook ledger. Examine what you spent money on during the past year and determine if it was tax deductible. If you missed any deductions you can always file an amended return. You may also be uncovering deductions for the current tax year as well.

DAY 4 DIARY

I am on my way to my financial breakthrough. Today I . . .

_____

_____

_____

_____

_____

_____

_____

_____

_____

_____

_____

_____

_____

_____

_____

_____

_____

_____

_____

Day
5

Acquire
Automatic Wealth

S	M	T	W	T	F	S
	1	2	3	4	⑤	6

✔ You are now almost halfway to your financial breakthrough. Today you will learn how much you should be saving each month and where to invest it. You will also learn how to put your savings and investment plan on auto-pilot. The key to day five is the ability to connect your goals with a success plan, and most importantly, a plan that requires little ongoing effort on your part.

WHAT YOU WILL NEED:

- Current figures on how much you currently have saved for retirement.
- Documents outlining any retirement plans that are available through your employer.
- Lump sum amounts for any financial goals you desire to reach (including retirement, college education, dream home, etc.).

- Account statements on your current investments so that you can determine how much you are earning now.

Cashing In

The amount of money that you can make will depend on how much time you have to reach your financial goals and what rate of return you will realize on your investments. Example: Two twin brothers each invest $50,000 at the age of thirty. One brother earns 12 percent while the other accepts a 6 percent return. Twenty-four years later at the age of fifty-four they meet to compare their results. The brother who had invested at a 6 percent rate has accumulated $200,000! This seems wonderful doesn't it? Sure, but the other brother invested at a 12 percent rate. Twenty four years later he has a whopping $800,000! This huge difference of $600,000 occurred simply as a result of earning 6 percent more!

Most of this book is about how to cut your expenses and make your money go further. The whole point of that process is to create a surplus. This surplus, or what is left over at the end of the month, is how you are going to build your financial independence. While there are many perspectives on retirement, my focus is on getting you to the point where you don't have to look to employment as your source of income. Consequently, I will not focus on "retirement" in the traditional sense, but will help you reach a point with your finances that allows you to be free from employment.

This freedom can be used in a variety of ways. Those choices are completely up to you after you reach your financial independence. Many people find this period of their life far more significant than just a time for leisure activities. Financial freedom provides a great opportunity for volunteer work, spending more time with family, and pursuing lifelong dreams. The bottom line is that in order to achieve financial freedom, a portion of your hard work each day must be invested toward that goal.

I have been teaching a simple and effective plan to my seminar audiences for years called "Automatic Wealth." The concept has been around for years, but I don't think anyone has ever presented it quite the way I have. As a financial teacher I

Get To The Point

The key to financial freedom is wisely investing your financial surplus.

have honestly been frustrated to find that most people lack the motivation to keep going after they begin their financial plan. So I determined that if I could help people put their investment plan on "auto pilot" they could make incredible progress without much ongoing effort. This is where the concept of automatic wealth became a reality. I know the concept works as people have shared countless stories with

me of how they were able to amass hundreds of thousands of dollars, even though they had never saved money before in their life. The concept is simple but effective.

Money Talk

Automatic investing plans draft money from a checking or savings account on a perpetual monthly basis until cancelled.

The automatic wealth principle simply requires that we determine how much money we need to invest each month to reach our goals and then set up an automatic funding plan that ensures this will be done. The plan must not require any ongoing effort.

BEGIN AT THE END

The first step is to start with a specific goal. Many people can only offer very vague ideas about what they want for their future. Skipping this crucial step is the critical point of failure and the reason why almost all Americans retiring today have little more than Social Security income during their senior years. What your future goals are is up to you, but you *must* be specific. This simple concept of setting a specific goal may seem like a small thing, but it can make a big difference.

By the way, I generally do not include Social Security in retirement planning. Assuming that it will still be around when you become eligible for benefits is risky. Depending on the amount of time until you reach retirement age, the program may no longer exist, or the benefits could be significantly reduced. However, if you want to include your Social Security in your retirement plans, you can obtain an estimate of your future benefits at www.ssa.gov.

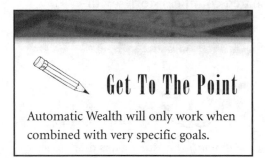

Get To The Point

Automatic Wealth will only work when combined with very specific goals.

If you are like most people, the idea of determining what lump sum you will need is far too abstract. You may not be able to imagine how much monthly income you will want ten, twenty, or thirty years down the road. What is easier to imagine is that *today* you are financially independent. You are at that point where you don't *have* to go out and earn a paycheck and can live comfortably. This is a very individual exercise and there is no "right answer."

Next, consider in today's dollars how much monthly income you would desire to have from your investments to reach that goal. While some people will live on substantially less during their years of financial independence, others will desire to pursue exotic travel and other activities that will require much more income to support. Your figures must be realistic based on how much time you have until that day, and what amount you currently have saved. To make this easy for you, you will find a list of on-line financial calculator services in the Internet Time Savers section of Day One. For the purposes of getting a general idea of where you are and how much you need to save, I have developed the following financial independence quick-reference chart.

FINANCIAL INDEPENDENCE QUICK REFERENCE CHART

Years until financial independence	Monthly savings required to accumulate $1,000 of future monthly income (adjusted for 3 percent inflation)
30	$130
25	$200
20	$310
15	$510
10	$930

The previous chart is based on the following assumptions:

- Inflation of 3 percent per year
- Average earnings on investment of 11 percent per year

Once the year of financial independence arrives, the income is distributed. In other words, you begin to receive monthly checks based on the amount you have invested. That distribution amount totals 8 percent of the account balance annually (the amount per year you counted on, plus enough to allow for the payment of taxes). Even if you earn 10 to 11 percent during your retirement, you should spend no more than 8 percent per year to allow for modest growth.

HOW TO USE THIS CHART

As an example, we will look at a person who wants $3,000 per month in today's dollars for their years of financial independence. This person is currently twenty five years away from their target date to quit working altogether. We know from the figures in the chart that for each $1,000 of future income they must save $200 per month. Since they need roughly $6,000 a month in future income, they must save $600 each month: $200 (for every $1,000) x 3. The lump sum actually accumulated in this example would be $945,000. Twenty-five years from now it will take $6,281 to purchase what we can purchase today for $3,000, due to inflation. With an annual distribution rate of 8 percent, monthly income generated would be $6,300. (Just what we need.)

This may seem somewhat confusing, but all we are doing is setting a goal and then adjusting that goal based on what goods and services will cost in the future. Wouldn't it be a shame if you set a goal to have $3,000 per month in income only to have it worth only half of that after factoring in inflation? This is why we must not only set a goal, we must also compensate for the rising cost of living as well.

What if an individual has more time—perhaps a total of thirty years? The required savings amount would then be only $390 a month: $130 (for every $1,000) x 3.

Money Talk

The term *tax shelter* is used to describe investments and accounts that offer special tax privileges.

TAX SHELTERS

Accounts that receive special tax privileges are referred to as tax shelters. (Benefits vary depending on account type.) These include company retirement plans (401ks) IRAs (both Roth and traditional), and annuities. It makes far more sense to take advantage of opportunities to allow your money to grow without being taxed. Also, within the context of a company retirement plan, you may be eligible for valuable matching benefits. This may be as generous as a dollar-for-dollar match by your employer, but is usually limited to 25 to 50 percent and then capped. In any case, allowing your money to grow tax deferred is benefit enough. The employer matching is icing on the cake.

The only time I am not enthusiastic about an employer plan is when the investment options are so limited that it would be unwise to invest in this manner. These are rare cases where individuals are only able to buy the company's own stock or have to choose between two or three mutual fund choices with horrible track records. It is only in these extreme circumstances that I would pass up what is otherwise an incredibly good investment and tax saving opportunity.

Use the following chart to prioritize where to invest your retirement savings.

RETIREMENT PLAN INVENTORY WORKSHEET

On this page you'll want to take an inventory of the retirement plans in which you and your spouse (if applicable) are participating. Although some of the plans listed below may not be familiar to you, most likely you will recognize the plans to which you belong. Once you're done, you may find that you need to do more to build up your retirement savings. If that appears to be the case, then you will want to adjust your monthly cash flow in a way that frees you to invest more money toward retirement savings.

YOU

	Amount Invested	Current Value	Years to Availability	Goal Amount
401(k)				
403(b)				
457				
IRA				
SEP-IRA				
KEOGH				
Annuity				
Other				

YOUR SPOUSE

	Amount Invested	Current Value	Years to Availability	Goal Amount
401(k)	_____	_____	_____	_____
403(b)	_____	_____	_____	_____
457	_____	_____	_____	_____
IRA	_____	_____	_____	_____
SEP-IRA	_____	_____	_____	_____
KEOGH	_____	_____	_____	_____
Annuity	_____	_____	_____	_____
Other	_____	_____	_____	_____

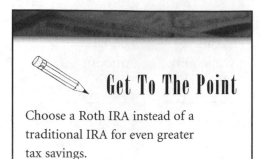

Get To The Point

Choose a Roth IRA instead of a traditional IRA for even greater tax savings.

The Roth IRA allows a maximum annual contribution of up to $3,000 in 2002, and even provides this benefit to a non-working spouse. In my analysis, there is almost no reason to utilize a traditional IRA since the Roth IRA offers such superior benefit. The primary difference between the new IRA and the older, traditional option is the tax benefit. The Roth IRA does not provide a current tax deduction for your contribution, but in exchange allows you to withdraw your money without any taxes during retirement. There is no question that it is a far greater benefit to be afforded the opportunity to withdraw all of your original deposits and your growth without taxation. This becomes more valuable the farther you are away from retirement since you have significant time to allow for compounding growth. See IRS publication 590 for more information.

Money Talk

Tax deferred simply means that you do not pay taxes until the money is withdrawn from the account. *Tax deductible* means that the amount you invest in the account is not included in your taxable income for that year. *Tax free* means that you are not required to pay taxes when the money is withdrawn.

Examples of each tax benefit:

- **Tax deferred**—Mutual fund annuities and fixed annuities.
- **Tax deferred and tax deductible**— Traditional IRAs (non Roth); Self Employed IRAs (SEP IRAs); 401k, 403b, 457k, and other company sponsored "qualified" plans.
- **Tax free (but not tax deductible)**— Roth IRAs and municipal bonds.

While I will not attempt to cover all of the IRA rules, since they are vast and involve a number of exceptions, suffice it to say that almost everyone who has earned income (and their non-working spouses) should be able to qualify for a Roth IRA. The rules get much stickier for the traditional IRA since the income requirements are significantly lower. Remember that even if you can qualify for the traditional IRA, I would still recommend the Roth.

You can also call the IRS at 800-829-1040 to request a free publication on IRA rules, or you may visit their Web site.

INTEGRATING YOUR RETIREMENT PLAN OPTIONS

A good question that you should be thinking about now is *where* to invest your money for your future financial independence. Not only what investment vehicles, but what type of tax shelter is most appropriate based on your circumstances.

The following graphic shows how to prioritize your tax sheltered investments.

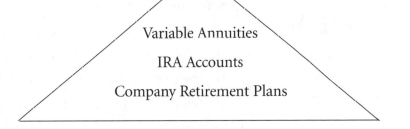

The most tax-efficient approach to building automatic wealth is to first fully fund any company retirement plan you have access to. Next, fund a Roth IRA (and if you are married, one for your spouse as well). Then, if you are still able to make additional investments, use a mutual fund annuity. A mutual fund annuity allows for unlimited annual contributions.

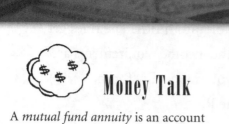

Money Talk

A *mutual fund annuity* is an account offered through insurance companies that allows you to invest in mutual funds without paying the taxes on your profits until you withdraw the money from your account (tax-deferred growth). Mutual fund annuities have no maximum contribution amounts.

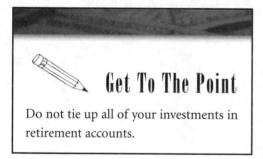

Get To The Point

Do not tie up all of your investments in retirement accounts.

Mutual fund annuities do not provide a tax deduction for contributing, but the growth inside the account is not taxed until it is withdrawn. In many states annuities are "creditor proof" assets which means that if you are sued, most courts cannot force you to pay the judgment from your annuity account. The annuity allows you to invest just like you would with a family of mutual funds. (Funds inside an annuity are technically called "sub accounts.") I recommend two products: American Skandia and Best of America. You cannot purchase either of these plans on your own; you must go through a broker.

Although the amount will vary from person to person, everyone should have some amount of ready cash available for an emergency. Many people suggest six months of your living expenses. I do not believe that this "emergency money" should necessarily be kept in a savings account or equivalent. I consider it perfectly appropriate to invest the money in a non-tax sheltered mutual fund account. This allows the money to grow and also allows you to get your hands on it in a couple of days if you need to. Keep in mind that if you invest in stock mutual funds the account will fluctuate in value, so you will have to consider that when determining how much you will need to have in your "emergency fund."

What should you do with your company retirement account when you change jobs? The best option when you change jobs is to transact a "direct rollover." This involves the following steps:

1. Open an IRA at a bank or brokerage firm. (The best choice.)
2. Contact your company's payroll and benefits department and request a direct rollover form.
3. Complete the direct rollover form by listing the location and account number of your new IRA account.
4. Wait about three weeks, and the money will automatically move from your company account to your new IRA.
5. Make investment choices based on available options.

It is important that you do not take direct possession of the funds prior to the deposit in your new IRA as this would trigger a 20 percent withholding requirement (your employer must send the IRS 20 percent of the account's value).

HOW TO INVEST YOUR MONEY

Money Talk

A *direct rollover* is a method of moving your retirement plan when you change jobs.

You must understand the difference between the type of account you may have and the investment selection that you make inside it. For years people have told me that they have their money "invested in an IRA." I inquire what investment they have in the IRA, and I usually get the same response: "It's invested in an IRA." The type of account you choose is a separate decision from where you will invest the money. You can make virtually all of the same investments in tax-sheltered accounts as in non-sheltered accounts. There are a few exceptions, but mutual funds, stocks, bonds, and all of the typical choices, are available one way or the other.

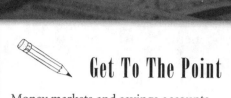

Get To The Point

Money markets and savings accounts pay low rates of return in exchange for a high degree of safety. These kinds of accounts are excellent choices for your short-term money or emergency reserve funds, but not the best option for growth.

MONEY MARKETS AND SAVINGS ACCOUNTS

If it were possible, would you like to take absolutely no risk and still enjoy an 11 to 12 percent rate of return? I would too! Unfortunately, that is not an available option. In order to enjoy these higher returns, you must be willing to accept the additional risk that comes along with them. The good news is that if you are a long-term investor, the risk is reduced since the stock market has averaged a return of 11 percent per year going back more than seventy-five years.

The term "average" can be misleading. In order to get the benefit of investing in the stock market, you must be willing to live with the daily or yearly ups and downs. Still, historically, there are many more "ups" than "downs."

One of the great benefits of using my automatic wealth approach is that it involves what is called "dollar cost averaging." What this means is that you will be adding money to your investments each month. Each time you add money, it automatically gets invested in the mutual funds that you have selected. Since you are buying every month, you are obtaining the average price of the stock or mutual fund over the course of each year. This means that you will never make the mistake of putting all of your money in on a day when the market is at its highest point. Since you are "averaging in," you will not need to be concerned about timing the market. You are buying incrementally over a long period of time, so you will not need to worry about picking the "right day" to get in.

The Financial Independence Quick Reference Chart that I utilized earlier in this chapter is based on an average annual return rate of 11 percent. To be able to earn this type of return in today's economy, you will have to invest your money in the stock market. This is an uncomfortable proposition for many people. If you do not want to take the risk that comes with this type of investing, you may want to consider other lower risk alternatives. Keep in mind that these lower risk

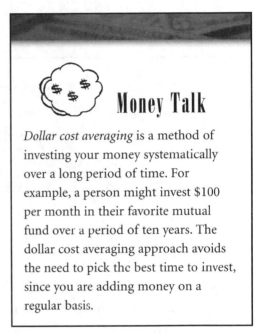

Money Talk

Dollar cost averaging is a method of investing your money systematically over a long period of time. For example, a person might invest $100 per month in their favorite mutual fund over a period of ten years. The dollar cost averaging approach avoids the need to pick the best time to invest, since you are adding money on a regular basis.

alternatives (like money markets and savings accounts) will offer lower returns. Lower returns will require that you save much more money each month to reach your goals.

Take Hesitant Harry, a thirty-year-old desiring a million dollars at retirement. He must save $356 per month earning an average annual return of 11 percent. Alternatively, at an 8 percent annual return, the amount jumps to $670! This is the reality of how compounding returns work. It is the reason that most people, despite how uncomfortable it may be for them, take some modest amount of risk.

Get To The Point

Use mutual funds to reduce risk but still enjoy stock market returns.

MUTUAL FUNDS

A mutual fund is an investment vehicle that combines the money of thousands of investors. The fund hires an investment manager or management team that selects the investments to be purchased for the fund. This approach allows investors to own a small piece of a substantial portfolio. "No-load" funds have no commissions attached to them. (For a list of no-load funds, see the appendix at the back of the book.)

Although mutual funds provide the unique opportunity for smaller investors to receive professional management and diversification, I believe that larger investors should also opt for mutual funds in lieu of picking their own stocks and bonds. The process of picking individual stocks is very complicated and time consuming. It also requires an ongoing daily monitoring that most people just don't have the time to keep up with. Unless you have professional assistance, I would highly recommend the mutual fund approach.

Money Talk

A *no-load mutual fund* is an investment that combines the money of thousands of investors, is managed by a professional, and has no commission.

My favorite mutual fund company is Invesco. You can reach them at (800) 525-8085 or on-line at www.invesco.com. Their minimum is only $50 to open an account and they have an automatic wealth system (electronic draft) that will work with your checking or savings account. You can get started today by downloading a prospectus and new account application from their Web site.

Invesco is a 100 percent no-commission fund group. Consequently, you will not be paying those pesky commissions that can be up to 8 percent of your initial deposit. They also have a significant number of fund choices. An additional benefit is their large selection of "sector funds." These are mutual funds that invest in one specific industry. You choose an industry, and then let the professional pick the individual stocks. As a professional money manager, I use the sector funds at Invesco as an integral part of all of my portfolios. I also appreciate their commitment to helping new investors. Their phone representatives and materials are extremely helpful for a beginning investor.

Other mutual fund groups worth consideration:

- Fidelity: 800-544-8888
- Vanguard: 800-662-7447
- T. Rowe Price: 800-225-5132
- Scudder: 800-621-1048
- Strong: 800-359-3379

(Web sites are listed at the end of the chapter.)

In most cases you will want to have at least $5,000 before taking the step of opening an account at a discount broker to buy mutual funds. Prior to having this amount of money, you should work with the funds directly. The advantage of using a discount broker is the opportunity to have all of your mutual funds in one account with one monthly statement. This even means that you can buy mutual funds from various fund families and still have them all in the same account. Years ago it would take weeks to move your money from one mutual fund family to another. Discount brokerage accounts allow these moves to take place in the course of one day. My favorite discount broker, and the one that I recommend for my clients, is Vanguard.

WHAT TYPE OF MUTUAL FUND IS RIGHT FOR YOU?

Mutual funds provide many approaches to investing. It is important for you to fully evaluate what risk you are willing to take in exchange for your expected return. This will be the beginning of your investing decision.

Corporate bond funds are a type of mutual fund that makes money by purchasing debt instruments of corporations. A *bond,* simply stated, is a loan that is made for a specific period of time at an agreed interest rate. *Corporate bonds* are a way of making money by loaning money to businesses. *Corporate bond funds* purchase a large number of bonds that involve a very diverse list of corporate borrowers. This provides you with protection should some of the bonds not pay off as agreed (known as default). The type of corporate bond fund you invest in will determine the rate of interest you are paid. Funds with higher rated bonds (bonds of larger more proven companies) have a higher rating and pay a lower interest rate.

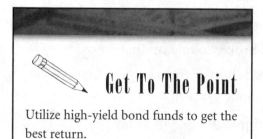

Get To The Point

Utilize high-yield bond funds to get the best return.

Bond funds containing bonds of less financially stable companies have a higher average interest rate, but present a greater risk. Some bond funds comprised of mostly lower rated bonds are called "junk bond funds" (also called high-yield bond funds). The term is really not a fair representation of what the quality of the bonds are. They are really just the second tier of quality and are not, as the name implies, of considerable risk of default. In fact, if you are strictly shopping for yield, you might find high yield bond funds a good choice. On average, most high yield bond funds experience only a 1 percent loss per year because of defaults. This is not a bad tradeoff when you are earning sometimes 3 to 4 percent above the yield of other corporate bond funds.

The experts agree that higher risk bonds should not be purchased individually but within the context of a fund. This gives you the opportunity of a higher yield but allows you to have your money spread out over a large number of corporations. The amount of diversification almost wipes out the risk entirely in the most well-managed funds.

The government issues the other general class of bond funds. Just as corporations issue bonds to borrow money, state and local governments—as well as the Federal Government—do too. The problem that we face investing in these kinds of bonds is the low rate of interest they pay. Depending on your

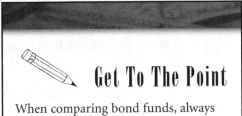

Get To The Point

When comparing bond funds, always compute the net after-tax return.

circumstances, you may be willing to earn a lower rate of return in exchange for the higher degree of safety. Another benefit of government bond funds is the tax advantages. Bonds issued by states are not subject to federal income tax and are usually free from that state's income tax (if applicable). If you live in a state with an income tax, you must buy a

bond fund with bonds issued by your state to get the "double tax free" benefit. Bonds issued by the federal government are free from local and state taxes. As a rule of thumb, the more secure the bonds in a fund, the lower the interest paid.

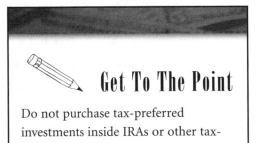

Get To The Point

Do not purchase tax-preferred investments inside IRAs or other tax-sheltered accounts.

The payments you receive from your bond fund (even if reinvested in the fund) will be considered income to you. Because of this you would be wise to find out how much you will "net" after taxes. Think about it this way: You need to compare oranges to oranges. For a person in the 28 percent tax bracket, a fund that earns 5 percent tax-free would be equivalent to a taxable 6.9 percent when you factor in the tax cost of the investment. The amount would be different for people in other brackets, so you may want to compute the after-tax yield for your particular situation. Visit www.tenday.com for my formula and help in determining the best bond fund for you. Of course it makes no sense to purchase tax-free bonds in accounts such as IRAs since they are already tax sheltered. (The only reason you would buy a lower-yield bond would be for the tax benefit. You are already getting that in the IRA.)

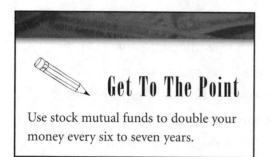

Get To The Point

Use stock mutual funds to double your money every six to seven years.

Although we have covered some basics on bond investing in this chapter, bonds are really not an adequate growth vehicle, even after adding in the tax benefits. If your goal is long-term growth, stock funds are really the only logical choice, although the idea makes the average person's heart pound a little more quickly. While it may seem a little scary, the reality of investing is that most people must earn double-digit returns.

Consider the following example: $10,000 invested earning 6 percent per year will grow to be $40,000 in twenty four years, while the same amount earning 12 percent grows to a whopping $160,000! Most people are not motivated by greed in making the decision to earn higher returns, but by necessity. They do not have enough time or money to accept lower rates of return. (Reality check: There is no such thing as a low-risk, high-yield investment, except in the land of wishful thinking.)

Investors in stock mutual funds enjoy a great variety of choices. I provide sample portfolios at www.tenday.com that are based on conservative, moderate, or aggressive growth. The following are reasonable expectations of what you can expect to see if you invest in a particular stock mutual fund risk level and examples of each:

Money Talk

The rule of 72 determines how long it will take to double your investment. Divide your earnings rate into 72 and you will know how many years it will require for your account to double. Example: If your return is 6 percent, it will take 12 years (72 divided by 6 = 12) to double; earn 9 percent and it will take 8 years (72 divided by 9 = 8).

Conservative: 10 to 12 percent average annual return (with the risk of losing 10 to 15 percent if the market is down).

Conservative mutual funds contain stocks of larger companies, also known as:

> *large cap funds;*
>
> *equity income;*
>
> *growth* and *income styles of management.*

For conservative investors, adding a bond fund will curb risk. For example, you might place 20 percent of a conservative portfolio in a bond fund and sacrifice one to two percent of your potential annual return.

Moderate: 12 to 15 percent annual return (with the risk of losing 12 to 15 percent if the market is down).

Moderate funds usually combine 50 percent of the types of funds in the conservative description with 50 percent *technology* and/or *aggressive growth styles,* also known as:

> *small cap funds;*
> *mid-cap funds.*

> Or *industry-specific funds,* also known as:
> *sector funds.*

Aggressive: 15 to 20 percent annual return (with the risk of losing 20 to 25 percent if the market is down).

Aggressive funds usually have a primary focus on *technology* and *aggressive growth styles* and also *sector funds.* Stock mutual fund figures are based on past history, but are no guarantee of future performance.

FUNDING YOUR CHILD'S COLLEGE EDUCATION

The method for funding your child's education is very similar to how you will approach funding your own financial independence. The difference is usually a shorter time frame for saving, and the amount of money required is substantially less. Again, only you can determine what your goals should be for funding your child's college education. In some families the plan is for Mom and Dad to pick up all of the college costs. In other cases the goal is to provide a percentage. Many families have also adopted a more practical approach to this whole issue, allowing for the possibility that their child may prefer vocational training in lieu of a traditional four-year college degree.

In any case, the process starts with your determination of a goal. If your child were eighteen today, how much would you desire to give him or her towards education? I have prepared the following quick-reference chart to give you some general ideas of college savings requirements. Also be sure to visit ChristianMoney.com for on-line college scholarship services.

COLLEGE FUND QUICK REFERENCE CHART

Age of Child	Monthly Savings Required for Every $10,000 Needed
Newborn	$25
Five Years Old	$42
Nine Years Old	$70
Thirteen Years Old	$145
Sixteen Years Old	$400

The above chart is based on the following assumptions:

·   Average annual return of 11 percent on money invested.
·   Inflation rate of 3 percent.

Example: Connie College, your sweet little newborn, will need $50,000 when she reaches the age of eighteen. You will need to save $125 every month: $25 (for every $10,000) x 5.

Example: You have a nine-year-old son and would like to provide $70,000 for his education when he is eighteen. You will need to save $525 every month: $70 (for every $10,000) x 7.

Get To The Point

Do not use Educational IRAs or Uniform Gift to Minors accounts.

WHERE TO INVEST

Saving for your child's college fund involves the same two major decisions you face when saving for your financial independence. First, you must determine what amount is needed. Second, you must determine where to invest the money.

The problem with the two most popular education-funding vehicles, Education IRAs and Uniform Gift to Minors accounts, is that they do not allow for any parental control. These accounts legally transfer complete control of the money to your child once they reach the age of majority in your state (usually 18). In my opinion, this is not a good plan and allows for a great number of very bad scenarios. My suggestion is to open an account with your name as the parent and simply "earmark" that account as the money for your child's educational pursuits.

Educational IRAs do provide the option of saving up to $500 per year and allows the money to grow without taxes. The money can be withdrawn tax free if used for education purposes. Perhaps one idea would be to establish an educational IRA and fund it with money your child receives from relatives (grandparents, aunts, uncles, etc.). You could then establish an account in your own name for the money that you are saving for your child. This will allow some access to the tax benefits of the education IRA, without putting your money at risk.

> **Money Talk**
>
> *Pre-paid college plans* provide the option of a fixed payment for a specified number of years and will guarantee a 2 or 4 year degree (usually at a college within your state).

Pre-paid college funds are another option (which are offered by many states and allow parents to invest in a college *within that state*), but in my opinion they are not the best choice. One reason is that your child cannot go to a school outside the state (without cashing in the plan and facing penalties in most states), and another is that there is little growth in those types of accounts. Other investments will provide you with greater returns and more educational choices.

Now that we have covered some of the keys to acquiring automatic wealth, use the following worksheet to plan your monthly contributions to each of your goals. Remember to include your retirement and funding for your children's education.

FINANCIAL GOAL WORKSHEET

Goal	Amount Required	Savings You Have Now	Monthly Savings Required

HOW TO GET STARTED BUILDING AUTOMATIC WEALTH

1. Decide what type of account(s) to use for your investments.
2. Determine how much you must invest each month to reach your goal(s).
3. Use an automatic draft arrangement to place your funding on auto-pilot.
4. Make a decision on how you will invest the money once it is inside your account.

 # INTERNET TIME SAVERS

www.christianmoney.com—Jim's recommended mutual fund allocations.

General Investment Education Sites

www.fool.com—Motley Fool

www.investorama.com—Investorama

www.smartmoney.com—Smart Money

www.money.com—Money Magazine

www.kiplingers.com—Kiplinger's Personal Finance

www.moneycentral.com—MSN Money Central

Investment Research

www.freeedgar.com—Provides Securities and Exchange Commission reports on public companies.

www.valueline.com—Value Line

www.wsrn.com—Wall Street Research Net

How to Start an Investment Club

www.better-investing.org—The National Association of Investment Clubs

On-line Brokers and Mutual Fund Companies

www.waterhouse.com—T.D. Waterhouse

www.ameritrade.com—Ameritrade

www.gomez.com—Gomez Advisors

www.americancentury.com—American Century

www.fidelity.com—Fidelity

www.invesco.com—Invesco

www.estrong.com—Strong

www.scudder.com—Scudder

www.vanguard.com—Vanguard

Stocks without a Broker or Commissions

www.netstockdirect.com—Net stock direct

www.dripcentral.com—Drip Central

FAST TRACK

1. The easiest way to acquire automatic wealth is to use "automatic investing." Open an investment account and request the automatic investing option. Most company retirement plans use this method and deduct designated amounts out of your paycheck for that purpose. Why not use

the same process with all of your investment accounts and put your investing completely on "auto pilot"?

2. Be sure that for each future financial goal you are investing a specific amount each month to achieve it. Use the Financial Independence or College Funding Quick Reference charts in this chapter.

3. The smartest way to build your investments for the future is utilizing tax shelters. Investing inside 401ks, IRAs, mutual fund annuities, and SEP IRAs allows your money to build much more rapidly as there are no taxes to pay until you withdraw it. Be sure to take full advantage of company retirement plans first, since they provide a tax deduction and tax-deferred growth. These plans also may feature company contributions as well.

4. Tax shelters are great, but don't overdo it! Most of these accounts are subject to IRS penalties if you take money out before retirement. It is a good idea to also keep some money in accounts not subject to these penalties.

5. The best way to invest is through mutual funds in the stock market. If you earn a 6 percent return, your money will double every twelve years. But earn 12 percent and it doubles every six! It is also wise to keep some money in risk-free investments like CDs, money markets, and saving accounts (in case of a financial emergency).

6. It is critical to match your investment experience and willingness to assume risk with the right investment choice. If you are more conservative, consider equity income mutual funds. If you are open to moderate levels of risk, a mixture of equity income funds and growth funds may be best. Those who are more tolerant of high risk and want the greatest potential growth should choose from sector funds and aggressive growth options.

7. Invest your children's college money aggressively if you have a long time-frame. The farther they are from the age of 18, the more you may justify being more aggressive in your mutual fund selections.

DAY 5 DIARY

I am on my way to my financial breakthrough. Today I . . .

_____

_____

_____

_____

_____

_____

_____

_____

_____

_____

_____

_____

_____

_____

_____

_____

_____

_____

Day 6

Correct Your Credit

S	M	T	W	T	F	S
	1	2	3	4	5	⑥

✔ This is the beginning of day six, and you are now halfway to your financial breakthrough! You should be making real progress by now. Today we will embark on the issue of credit. You will learn how to obtain your credit reports, understand the full effect credit can have on your finances, become aware of your credit rights under Federal law, and learn how to use those rights to improve your credit file.

WHAT YOU WILL NEED:

- Copies of your credit report from the three major credit bureaus.
- Any letters you have received from lenders declining credit.

This chapter is not about debt. That was covered on day three. Many people mistakenly confuse the issue of "credit worthiness" with debt. Although these two topics are close cousins, they comprise very different elements of your personal financial health. Your credit report is a record of how much debt you have, debt you have had in the past, and your payment history. Specifically, it records how timely you have made your payments. Additionally, public records are also a part of your report. These would include judgments, bankruptcies, and IRS tax liens (and in some cases state tax liens as well).

CHRISTIAN MONEY PRINCIPLE

Paying bills on time is a critical part of good stewardship. If you are unable to pay your debts as agreed, you should communicate with your creditors and work out a plan that allows for you to get caught up. *The wicked borroweth, and payeth not again: but the righteous sheweth mercy, and giveth* (Psalm 37:21 KJV).

Your credit history determines your ability to borrow money and at what interest rate. All major lenders will judge your credit worthiness on the basis of information that is compiled and maintained by organizations known as credit bureaus. These bureaus, which are for-profit enterprises, make money by charging their members a fee. Members of credit bureaus have access to information other member organizations have reported about consumers. They also can report information about your payment history with their firm. Corporations have credit records too. If you have incorporated your business, it is likely that it has a credit record that is separate from your personal report.

HOW TO OBTAIN COPIES OF YOUR CREDIT REPORT

For many people obtaining a copy of their credit report seems like a totally pointless exercise. After all if you have bad credit, you have bad credit. Right? Not necessarily. In surveys I have conducted during my seminars throughout America, I have discovered that people find errors in their credit report nearly 50 percent of the time. What is even more disturbing is the wide-sweeping effects that bad credit can have on one's personal life. Having bad credit can cause you difficulty in getting approved for loans or credit cards and can cause you to pay higher interest rates. To make matters even worse for those who are struggling, even renting an apartment can be a very difficult process with blemishes on one's credit.

Cashing In

"A penny saved is a penny earned." What does that have to do with your credit report? The state of your credit report *directly* affects your ability to borrow money and what interest rate you qualify for. Improving your credit could easily save more than a thousand dollars per year in interest. One thousand dollars per year invested at 11 percent would be worth $64,202 in 20 years! Here's a bonus: Many employers check credit backgrounds prior to making hiring decisions, so having a great credit file might even lead to more money in the workplace too.

All three credit bureaus (listed below) are required by law to provide you with a free copy of your credit report any time you have been denied credit based on information that they provided to a lender. Typically when a letter is sent to you declining your request for a loan or credit card, it will say which credit bureau(s) provided the information. Additionally, Experian (formerly called TRW) provides a free credit report one time per year, just for the asking. If you haven't been denied credit and would like a credit report from the other two companies, Equifax and Trans Union, contact them by mail or Internet (and be prepared to pay up to $8.50 per copy, depending on your state).

(You will find links to all of the credit bureaus and downloads for all the sample letters in this chapter at www.tenday.com.)

Equifax
P.O. Box 740241
Atlanta, GA 30374-0241

www.equifax.com

Experian (formerly TRW)
P.O. Box 949
Allen, TX 75013-0949

www.experian.com

Trans Union
Consumer Disclosure Center
P.O. Box 390
Springfield, PA 19064-0390

www.tuc.com

One useful resource on the Internet that I recommend is www.creditreport-net.com which provides a detailed credit report that merges data from all three bureaus for $29.95. The service is convenient and can provide you with an immediate on-line report. They also offer a subscription service for $49.95 per year, which gives you a merged credit report every quarter.

Money Talk

The *Fair Credit Reporting Act* is a Federal law that provides you with specific rights regarding issues that affect your credit record.

YOUR RIGHTS REGARDING CREDIT BUREAUS

- Information older than seven years old must be removed. (Chapter 7 bankruptcy may stay on as long as ten years.)
- Incorrect information must be removed.
- Information that cannot be verified with the creditor must be removed.
- At your request, a one hundred-word statement explaining a credit item must be included.
- At your request, positive information that is missing from your report must be added (sometimes for a small fee).
- The Federal Trade Commission can be contacted to report credit bureau problems.
- Use small claims court to sue the credit bureau if they do not follow the law.

Once you receive your credit report, it is critically important to make the distinction between bad credit which has been correctly reported to the credit bureaus, and disparaging information that is erroneous. Make a list of any negative items (slow pays, charge-offs, etc.) and determine if any of these are older than seven years. Next, write a letter to each credit bureau challenging the items in question. Use the following letter:

SAMPLE LETTER: REMOVING OLD CREDIT ITEMS

Attention Credit Report Data Management Department:

I have just reviewed my credit report and have noticed that the following items which are older than seven years are appearing on my report:

(Insert items in question here.)

Based on the Fair Credit Reporting Act, the statute of limitations on these items has expired. I request the immediate deletion of these items from my report and that you send me an updated copy of my credit report to the address listed below.

Your Name
Your Address
Your Social Security Number

Get To The Point

Incorrect information on your credit report must be removed by the credit bureau within thirty days.

You will notice as you review each creditor account that there are typically several items of information to be considered. The current balance, the highest balance you had, any incidents of lateness, and the current status of the account (currently on time or in arrears, etc.). In theory, it is the responsibility of the credit bureau to report accurate information. The reality is that credit bureaus rely on the information that they receive from member companies.

These are very large institutions attempting to communicate with each other, which is not always an easy task. Although this may sound like a liability for you as a consumer, it can actually be used to your advantage. Since it is highly unlikely that each and every aspect of the negative items on your report will be accurate, it gives you a basis for challenging the item altogether. For example, a credit account that you have been late on a couple of times may appear with the wrong current balance. On this basis, you could then dispute the item as being inaccurate and potentially have the entire account removed from your report or at a minimum the negative history removed. This is very likely if the account is now paid or if the negative history occurred more than a year ago. Use the following letter to challenge incorrect information on your credit report.

SAMPLE LETTER: REMOVING INCORRECT ITEMS

Attention Credit Report Data Management Department:

I have just reviewed my credit report and have noticed that the following credit accounts contain incorrect information:

(Insert items in question here.)

Based on the Fair Credit Reporting Act, this information must be verified for accuracy within thirty days. I request either a correction to these inaccuracies or the immediate deletion of these items from my report. Please send me an updated copy of my credit report to the address listed below.

> Your Name
> Your Address
> Your Social Security Number

CONFRONTING NEGATIVE INFORMATION

If there is negative information on your credit report, it is your right to have that item removed within thirty days if the credit bureau cannot substantiate the information. The issue is a legal one. Congress wrote the law governing credit bureaus. Since we must accept the negatives of it (for instance, if you file for bankruptcy, it stays on your credit report for ten years) I don't see a thing wrong with forcing the credit bureaus to live up to the full regulatory scope of the rules. You can question any information on your report. If the credit bureau can not live up to its requirements—responding to you within thirty days—they must remove the information from the report. In fact, I think it is clear that Congress was allowing this "loophole" of forced verification (within thirty days or required removal) to give an incentive to the credit bureaus to keep their records accurate and timely. It was obviously not enough, as most studies show that 40 percent or more of credit reports contain inaccuracies and unverifiable data.

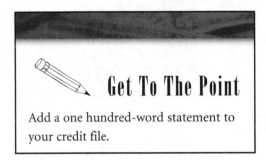

Get To The Point

Add a one hundred-word statement to your credit file.

It is a common occurrence for people to find themselves with bad credit as a result of a one-time catastrophic event. This could be an unexpected medical problem, death in the family, or other tragedy. Creditors are people, too, and can be understanding if you give them a chance. These kinds of circumstances are perfect examples of times to utilize the one hundred-word statement strategy.

This provision in the Fair Credit Reporting Act is not appropriate for people who have had chronic credit problems for years. It is also not likely that a "dog ate my homework" type of explanation will do you much good. If you have a legitimate one-time circumstance that has caused you to get behind on your credit accounts, you should definitely use this strategy. I would suggest that you employ this strategy after you have done your best to get the items in question removed completely by utilizing the prior techniques in this chapter. It is also best to add the one hundred-word statement once you are back on time with your creditors. The letter would then outline the problem and conclude with the information that you are now on time with your payment obligations. Most creditors would not be likely to have much mercy on you if you appear to still be behind in your payments.

Use the following letter to have a one hundred-word statement added to your credit file.

SAMPLE LETTER: ADDING A ONE HUNDRED-WORD STATEMENT

Attention Credit Report Data Management Department:

I am requesting that the attached statement be added to my credit report corresponding with [account name and number]. Based on the Fair Credit Reporting Act, this statement should be furnished to all creditors who request my credit report.

Please send me an updated copy of my credit report including my statement to the address listed below.

> Your Name
> Your Address
> Your Social Security Number

As Murphy's Law suggests, often anything that can go wrong, will go wrong. Many times those items that you have paid faithfully over the years do not show up on one or more of your credit reports. A perfect

Get To The Point

Add positive information that is missing from your credit report.

example of this involves a client I was working with. He had a mortgage with a local bank in his hometown. The way the loan was structured, it was considered a "portfolio loan," or an internal loan of the bank rather than a traditional mortgage which would usually be arranged by the bank and then funded by an outside source. Consequently, the loan was not being reported on my client's credit report. This large loan, which he had always paid on time, was a jewel in his credit crown and was nowhere to be found when he was in need of a low-interest rate auto loan.

Credit bureaus are allowed to charge you a fee for their expenses to add items that are missing. These fees are very reasonable and may only amount to few dollars to cover their postage and phone calls. Use the following letter to have positive information added to your credit file:

SAMPLE LETTER: ADDING MISSING INFORMATION

Attention Credit Report Data Management Department:

I have just reviewed my credit report, and I am requesting that the following item(s) be added:

(Insert items in question here.)

Based on the Fair Credit Reporting Act, this information should be added upon request within thirty days. Please send me an updated copy of my credit report to the address listed below.

> Your Name
> Your Address
> Your Social Security Number

As with any set of rules or laws, there is always the question of what one should do when the rules are not followed. There have been many famous legal judgments awarded to consumers against creditors and credit bureaus. In fact, credit bureaus in years past have been subject to multi-million-dollar fines from state

Money Talk

The *Federal Trade Commission* is the United States Government agency that enforces the rules for how credit bureaus operate.

regulators for not following the credit laws. I would recommend from the outset that you mail all of your letters to the credit bureaus by certified mail with a return receipt for your records. I would set up a file with all of your credit information and keep a copy of all correspondence and proof of delivery.

If your legal requests go without proper attention, I would recommend you send a letter indicating that you will make a formal complaint to the Federal Trade Commission if the law is not followed. Regulation of credit bureaus is one of the major functions of the FTC. If things get to that point, you can write to the Federal Trade Commission at:

Federal Trade Commission
Consumer Response Center-240
Washington, D.C. 20580
www.ftc.org (for filing on-line complaints)

The whole idea of going to court can seem very intimidating. However, an easy and low-cost way to get justice is to file a small claims lawsuit. Small claims court is a local county court that provides a venue for lawsuits that involve amounts below a certain maximum. Most small

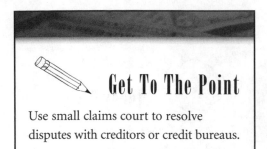

Get To The Point

Use small claims court to resolve disputes with creditors or credit bureaus.

claims courts have maximum awards of between $3,000 and $5,000. You may be required to sue for a certain amount even if all you want is just for your credit report to be cleared up. In this case, you may have to demonstrate "damages."

If you have been turned down for credit or a job, or paid a higher interest rate than you would have otherwise, these facts should be used when you go to court. You may also find that many small claims courts allow for "equity judgments." This is not a judgment for money, but an order from the court for a defendant to take certain steps to correct a situation. For example, you might get an order from a judge that an item be removed from your credit file. This would not mean any money to you, but would force the creditor to live up to correcting the problem.

You do not need an attorney, and in most jurisdictions a small claims case cost you less than $50. The format of small claims court is very informal. In fact, you may want to go and watch your local small claims court prior to your own case coming before the judge. Most often the judge will simply ask each side to tell their story and present their evidence. In many cases the judge will rule right on the spot.

The interesting thing I have learned is that when a lawsuit involving credit issues is filed in small claims court, often the matter never goes to trial. What frequently happens is that once the credit bureau or creditor is served your lawsuit and a summons, they will contact you to work things out. A consumer suing a creditor or credit bureau does not bring good publicity for these organizations, and the sooner they can settle things with you the better for them. I am not in any way suggesting that you file a frivolous lawsuit, but if your rights are being violated you must stand up and fight for yourself.

CREDIT SCORES

In the "old days," credit decisions by lenders were made by human beings. It was likely that a credit application would be reviewed by at least two people prior to a decision to grant a loan being made. In the case of larger loans, they would go through a "loan committee." While there still are "layers" of approval, much of the process is based on a mathematical calculation known as your credit score. A computer software program reviews your entire credit history, and then you are assigned a numeric score. This score will be the basis for what interest rate you pay or whether you qualify for a loan at all. For more information on credit scoring and to obtain your credit score, go to www.creditscoring.com. Of course, the more negative items you have removed from your credit report, the higher your score will go, so don't get discouraged.

Your credit report is a record of your current loan balances, and your payment history on your debts. It also contains public record information about you such as judgments and bankruptcies.

The Fair Credit Reporting Act is the law that specifically regulates how credit bureaus operate. This includes how long they can keep certain information on file and with whom they can legally share this information. It also provides you with conditions upon which information must be removed. You can make a complaint directly to this organization if the credit bureau is not following the rules in your case.

INTERNET TIME SAVERS

Credit Bureaus

www.equifax.com—Equifax

www.experian.com—Experian (formerly TRW)

www.tuc.com—Trans Union

Credit Scores

www.creditscoring.com

Credit Reports On-line

www.creditreport-net.com

www.freecreditreport.com

FAST TRACK

1. Your credit history affects more than just your ability to borrow money. It will also determine what interest rate you pay and can even be the difference in getting your next job.
2. There are three major credit bureaus. In order to know the true condition of your credit, you must obtain your credit report from all three credit bureaus.
3. The Fair Credit Reporting Act provides you with certain rights concerning your credit. Among these rights are the ability to have incorrect or old information removed and even

the opportunity to add a one hundred-word explanation. You can also force the credit bureau to add any positive information that may be missing.

4. The Federal Trade Commission is the government agency that regulates credit bureaus.

5. Most lenders make their lending decisions based on a *credit score* rather than a subjective judgment.

6. Be sure to obtain your credit score to determine the real state of your credit. You can access your credit score on the Internet.

7. You arc entitled to a free copy of your credit report any time you are denied credit based on information that the credit bureau provides. Experian provides one free credit report per year just for the asking.

8. You have the right to sue the credit bureau in small claims court if they do not comply with the provisions of the Fair Credit Reporting Act.

9. Use the letters in this chapter to dispute negative items on your credit report.

DAY 6 DIARY

I am on my way to my financial breakthrough. Today I . . .

_____

_____

_____

_____

_____

_____

_____

_____

_____

_____

_____

_____

_____

_____

_____

_____

Day 7

Investigate Your Insurance, Part 1

✔ This is day seven, and our next step is to evaluate an important area that I hope you will seldom have to use: Insurance. Today you will learn the basics of insurance, how much insurance you really need, how to cancel insurance that is unnecessary, and how to cut your overall insurance costs while at the same time obtaining more effective coverage. Insurance is such a significant part of our personal financial lives that, in order to deal with the topic, I have dedicated two days of your financial breakthrough to it.

WHAT YOU WILL NEED:

- Life insurance policy(s).
- Health insurance policy(s).

- All other insurance documents such as mortgage insurance, credit life insurance, cancer insurance, disability insurance, etc.

Cashing In

The amount of money saved on life and health insurance can be substantial. It would not be unreasonable to expect to reduce your ongoing insurance costs by 30 percent or more. You will also be able to buy more insurance for the same money. This means that if the primary breadwinner in your family is currently underinsured, you can gain peace of mind by remedying that. Consider this example: If you are able to save $400 per year on insurance, it could grow to an extra $25,000 for retirement or your children's college fund!

An interesting phenomenon occurs with the area of insurance that involves a complete reliance on false information. It's kind of like the story of the circus elephant. Circus elephants are restrained immediately after birth with a chain connected to a simple stake in the ground. The young elephant may try to challenge the restraint but learns quickly that it is more than enough to hold him. What is amazing is that when the elephant grows bigger and stronger (and develops the ability to easily defeat the restraint) he does not even try. Early in his life the elephant developed the belief that he could not free himself from the chain. As a mature elephant he accepts the control of the chain without question. It may seem ridiculous to think of a six-ton animal being controlled with such minimal restraints, but that is what misconceptions learned early in life can do.

We humans can fall victim to the very same thing. Michael Schwartz calls it "limiting the area of the possible." I couldn't agree more with his description. We become especially vulnerable to false beliefs regarding insurance. For instance: 1) Most companies charge about the same for the comparable coverage; 2) It is OK to skimp on insurance; 3) Once you get a policy, you shouldn't ever have to go back and check on rates; 4) You need a lot of specialized coverage . . . just in case.

CHRISTIAN MONEY PRINCIPLE

It is imperative that you adequately provide for your family, especially in the event of a major illness or even the death of the family's primary breadwinner. *People who don't take care of their relatives, and especially their own families, have given up their faith. They are worse than someone who doesn't have faith in the Lord* (1 Timothy 5:8 CEV).

You may have bought insurance believing one or more of these myths. I find it amazing that the same people who shop multiple grocery stores to save a few cents on produce, will needlessly pay thousands of dollars for insurance they don't need or overpriced policies. The truth is that they don't ever question the rates they are paying or the bottom-line purpose for having the coverage in the first place. Is it possible to save money on our insurance coverage and still be responsible? Is it possible to get more coverage for less money? Absolutely! During the next two days, you will learn exactly how to do it.

GETTING STARTED

By now you may have compiled a fairly large stack of dusty insurance policies to review (perhaps for the first time since you received them). It is important that you begin organizing them and making a list of what you have. Use the chart on the next page to get organized, and then we will continue. Be sure to discard or file in a separate filing area any old policies that are no longer active. You may find that as you have changed insurance coverage over the years, your policies have been updated, or you have received additional insurance contracts. To make things simple, find the policies that are currently in force. Look at the issue date of the policy, found within the first few pages of your insurance contract. If you have more than one copy of your policy, you should use the one with the *most recent* issue date.

PERSONAL INSURANCE INVENTORY

Policy Type	Annual Premium	Details of Coverage

Policy Type: List auto, homeowner's, health, life, or other category of insurance you are referencing. (We will be covering auto, homeowners, and liability insurance tomorrow, but you should still list them on this chart for quick reference.)

Annual Premium: You may need to get out your bank statements to determine this. Some insurance contracts are paid annually while others are paid quarterly or even monthly. It is important that you know what your annual cost is so you have a benchmark for comparison.

Details of Coverage: Although insurance polices are not easy to read, most have what is known as a "declarations page." This is usually within the first three or four pages and provides a summary of your benefits. Of course you should always read the entire policy to uncover all the details and potential hidden loopholes in the coverage. For today we will only need a general overview of the coverage.

Your chart may have an entry like this:

Policy Type	Annual Premium	Details of Coverage
Auto	$350	$100 deductible; liability $300,000 per accident and $100,000 per person for medical

While this may seem confusing now, we will define all the terms later. Don't worry if you don't understand what everything means. Just do the best that you can and write down a basic overview of what is on each declaration page of your insurance policies.

RISK MANAGEMENT

The very first concept you must come to grips with on the subject of insurance is risk management. We all face risk in our daily lives and can deal with it in a variety of ways. In

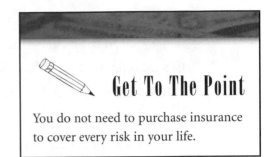

Get To The Point

You do not need to purchase insurance to cover every risk in your life.

the financial planning field, we define these risk management choices in three ways:

Risk Avoidance. This is the simple concept of identifying a risk and then avoiding it. I typically practice risk avoidance in the area of safety. Although I love motorcycles, I have not owned one in ten years. Because they involve higher risk than some other forms of transportation, I have chosen to give up that experience to avoid the potential dangers. (I have a wife and three children to think about.) Not everyone would, or should, make that same decision, but it is one that I decided to make for my situation. One of the best examples of risk avoidance is deciding not to smoke or take other needless health risks. (While there are many risks that we can choose to avoid, some are unavoidable. That's life.)

Risk Transfer. Transferring risk, or what is commonly known as insurance, is one of the most popular ways to prepare for the unpredictable and sometimes unavoidable crises of life. Will we live to the age of 90, or die at a youthful 35? Will we have a safe drive to the office or be involved in a vehicle accident? Will we have a generally healthy life or incur substantial medical expenses? Is the home that we live in safe from danger ,or will it be burglarized or destroyed by fire? These questions are real and important to consider. Without a doubt, these concerns are just cause for creating reasonable contingency plans

141

since the future is potentially filled with these risks. These are valid issues that in most cases must be dealt with by purchasing insurance. In this manner, for a specific price we transfer our potential risk to another entity—the insurance company.

Risk Retention. Risk retention is the concept of being "self-insured" or otherwise not attempting to purchase insurance to protect against a particular risk. This is a completely foreign concept to most consumers. Many of us feel we need to be protected against every risk imaginable, leaving us easy targets for one insurance scam after the next. There are some insurance salespeople who excel at pointing out obscure risks to a consumer and coming up with a form of insurance to cover it, resulting in unnecessary insurance coverage. The point is that you cannot afford to insure against every possible risk in your life. You must carefully decide which risks you can self-insure, and which are too great and must be transferred to an insurance company in the form of purchasing a policy.

Probably the most ridiculous form of insurance is called "dread disease" coverage. In fact, many states have banned the sale of this type of insurance altogether. It would include specialized insurance for just about every disease one can imagine including heart disease, diabetes, and cancer. These plans are all simply duplicate coverage if you already have health insurance.

Money Talk

Dread disease insurance is banned by many states. It is insurance that provides benefits only if you become afflicted with a *specific* disease such as diabetes or cancer.

INSURANCE YOU DO NOT NEED:

Cancer insurance—Duplicates service provided by health insurance.

Accident insurance—Duplicates service provided by health insurance.

Mortgage insurance—Provides enough money to pay off the mortgage in the event of your death. (The purchase of additional term life insurance would give the same result at about half the cost.)

Credit life insurance—Provides enough money to pay off any outstanding debts in the event of your death, and is usually sold in conjunction with a consumer loan or even a credit card. Again, purchase enough simple term life insurance. Credit life insurance can cost more than ten times that of simple term life.

DISABILITY INSURANCE

I am not a proponent of disability insurance because it is very expensive and can be extremely difficult to collect on. After all, proving that you are disabled and forcing an insurance company to pay up are not always easy propositions. In the case of life

Money Talk

Term life insurance is the simplest form of life insurance. The policyholder pays an agreed annual premium and, when the insured dies, the amount of the death benefit is paid to the beneficiary.

insurance, there is indisputable evidence that the coverage is needed. Not so with a disability. If, despite the potential pitfalls, you decide to pursue disability insurance, at least choose a policy with a six-month waiting period. You would not be eligible to receive payments until you have been disabled for at least six months, but you will pay substantially lower rates than for policies with waiting periods of thirty and sixty days.

Money Talk

Nursing home insurance, or what is commonly known as *long term care,* provides coverage against the risk of incurred expenses associated with a lengthy nursing home stay. Although most people think of this as something that could only happen when they are older, younger people who are disabled may also find themselves in a nursing home.

Money Talk

Travel insurance is available in two forms. First there are life insurance policies sold at airports that cover *that specific flight only.* Another form of travel insurance is *trip cancellation* coverage. This form provides you with the ability to cancel your trip and be reimbursed or have the ability to reschedule it (depending on the policy).

NURSING HOME INSURANCE

Nursing homes are *not* hospitals, which means that your health insurance may not pay the bill. If you are chronically ill and/or elderly, at some point you may need twenty-four-hour-a-day medical assistance and supervision. This kind of care can be expensive. The solution being offered by the insurance industry is a special kind of coverage known as "long term care" or nursing home insurance. This coverage is a close cousin to disability, but has significant differences. I do not want to dismiss this policy altogether, but I do have some of the same concerns as with disability coverage. The policy premiums are expensive. Consequently, I believe it would be better to invest the money and "self insure." In other words, build up your net worth to the point that your own investments would be sufficient to cover the expense of a nursing home. If you do decide to purchase long term care insurance, my general principles will apply to this form of coverage as well.

TRAVEL INSURANCE

Another popular and overpriced form of insurance is travel insurance. This is an unnecessary expense if you have the appropriate amount of life insurance. Furthermore, some credit card companies offer free travel insurance if you purchase your airline ticket using their account. Also, many travel agents now offer travel insurance as a free "perk" for their high-mileage customers.

A second common mistake while traveling is to purchase insurance on a rented vehicle. This coverage can be very expensive and is usually a complete waste of money. First of all, you should determine if your primary auto insurance policy provides coverage for you while driving a rental car. If it doesn't, move your business elsewhere. If you are like me and carry a high deductible and are concerned about the first $1,000 of potential damage while renting a vehicle, use a credit card that provides free insurance that will offset your deductible.

One situation where travel insurance might be a wise choice is if you are in questionable health and are investing a significant amount in a special cruise or other travel package. In this case you may want to consider "trip cancellation coverage." It will probably cost as much as 10 percent of the travel package, but it will provide you with the opportunity to reschedule if you become ill prior to travel. Only use this type of coverage if you are in these special circumstances.

Get To The Point

Say no to expensive extended warranties.

EXTENDED WARRANTIES

Extended warranties are another form of unnecessary and overpriced insurance. With a few rare exceptions, I believe that extended warranty plans are a bad deal for the consumer. First, if you were to simply save the money normally spent on warranties covering everything from your television set to your refrigerator, you would amass a small fortune that you could establish as your own "self-insurance fund." Secondly, many of these warranties are completely useless. The contracts are filled with requirements and exclusions so difficult to comply with that you need an attorney to make a claim. What is even more fraudulent about many of these warranties is that some simply duplicate the existing manufacturer's warranty, which is free when you purchase the product.

Money Talk

Pre-paid legal services provide low-cost access to attorneys. Not legally considered to be "insurance," these services could be viewed as an HMO for legal needs. Provider law firms fulfill a wide array of legal services for a small monthly fee.

LEGAL INSURANCE

One form of insurance that falls outside the mainstream is legal insurance. In the beginning days of legal insurance, the product was very weak. However, in recent years the industry has made huge progress. These plans typically have a low monthly fee and provide unlimited phone consultations with attorneys, along with a myriad of other included benefits. Some have even gone so far as to provide legal representation during IRS audits. All in

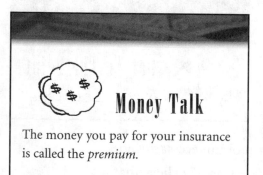

Money Talk

The money you pay for your insurance is called the *premium*.

all, it is a very good value for the money. You can learn more by going to www.christianmoney.com and entering the legal resources area.

CANCEL UNNECESSARY INSURANCE POLICIES

Depending on whether you have paid insurance premiums in advance, you may be entitled to a refund when you cancel a policy.

Obviously, the first order of business is to identify any insurance coverage you do not need. Canceling may not be as simple as discontinuing the premium payments. I recommend that you send a letter (certified with a receipt is best) to cancel your coverage. In some cases you will determine that you have prepaid your

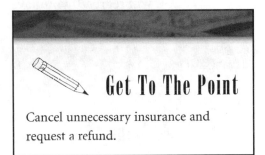

Get To The Point

Cancel unnecessary insurance and request a refund.

insurance for several years in advance. The most common example of this is credit life insurance. Often this insurance is financed with the item you purchased (car loans, appliances, etc.). In cases like this, you may have not only paid more than ten times too much for this insurance, you may be paying interest charges on top of that! The good news is that you should be entitled to a refund of any *unused* premium.

For example, you may have paid for three years of coverage and may only be in the first year. In this case, you could potentially be entitled to a refund check of several hundred dollars (depending on the type of coverage).

Another important note on credit life insurance is that most states strictly prohibit lenders from requiring it. If you were told you had to purchase credit life insurance to get approval for a loan, you may have grounds for a complete refund of the entire amount. In any case, I can tell you that my students regularly rush home after my seminars and are able to generate significant amounts of refunds by canceling unneeded insurance. Not only are you reducing future expenses, in many cases you are able to put cold, hard cash in your pocket within a few days.

Canceling insurance is a big decision, so don't rush into a decision you will regret. If you have thought it through and have concluded that the insurance in question is unnecessary, then go ahead and cancel it. Be careful to make your cancellation decisions within the overall context of your insurance plan. For example, if you decide to cancel your credit life insurance policies and replace them with term life insurance, you should wait until the term life insurance has been purchased before you cancel your current coverage.

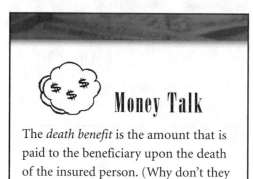

Money Talk

The *death benefit* is the amount that is paid to the beneficiary upon the death of the insured person. (Why don't they just call it death insurance?)

NECESSARY INSURANCE—AND HOW TO BUY IT INEXPENSIVELY

The following forms of insurance are essential for most people:

- Life
- Health
- Homeowner's or Renter's
- Auto
- Personal liability

If you are in business, you may need additional forms of commercial and professional liability coverage. This chapter will only cover non-business forms of insurance. If you are in business, you should visit with your insurance agent about commercial coverage issues.

LIFE INSURANCE: WHO SHOULD BUY IT?

In my years in practice, I have found the area that causes the most confusion in the whole realm of financial planning is life insurance. The life insurance industry has developed excellent sales tactics and has adopted the view that everyone

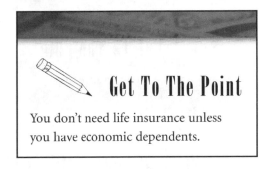

Get To The Point

You don't need life insurance unless you have economic dependents.

needs life insurance. Furthermore, they have really crossed an ethical boundary by selling life insurance as an investment. In this section I will help you determine if you need life insurance, how much you need, and what form of coverage is best.

If you are single, or if you are married and both you and your spouse work, you may not need life insurance at all. I know that this may strike you as a totally foreign concept. (After all doesn't *everyone*

need life insurance?) I am amazed at the large number of single individuals that carry significant amounts of life insurance. In one case, a single person told me that he had a one million-dollar policy that would go to his mother if he died. Although he was not supporting his mother financially,

Money Talk

A *rider* is an addendum to your life insurance policy that allows coverage to additional family members.

he thought it would be "nice" for her to receive this lump sum if he died. This may sound like a perfectly admirable gesture, and you may wonder what the problem was with him doing this. The bottom line: He was not investing anything for the future because he spent his entire surplus on insurance he didn't need. What I usually find is that people become "insurance poor" and end up with nothing left to invest. As we have discussed, investing surplus is the key to long-term financial success.

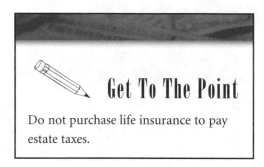

Get To The Point

Do not purchase life insurance to pay estate taxes.

WHO DOESN'T NEED LIFE INSURANCE?

Single Individuals—The exception is if you have children and need to provide for their future.

DINKs (Double Income No Kids)—If both spouses are working and capable of providing for themselves financially.

Children—Unless your child brings home a big paycheck to help support the family. Many families desire a small policy in the amount of $10,000 that would provide enough money for burial costs. Rather than purchasing a separate policy, it is much less expensive to simply add your child to your policy through what is called a "rider." Most life insurance policies allow for children to be added in minimal amounts for this very purpose.

Independently Wealthy Individuals—Once your net worth reaches a significant amount, you probably don't need life insurance. Specifically, if the value of your estate surpasses the amount your family would need for ongoing support, no life insurance is needed. Strangely enough, this group is probably the most frequently targeted by life insurance salesmen. The reason they are told to buy life insurance is to pay the estate taxes for their children. Keep in mind that one spouse can leave the other an unlimited amount of assets without any estate taxation. The issue being dealt with here is the estate taxes owed prior to the estate being distributed to children or other beneficiaries. Recent legislation has substantially increased the exemption

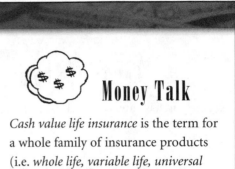

Money Talk

Cash value life insurance is the term for a whole family of insurance products (i.e. *whole life, variable life, universal life*, etc.) which are the more expensive counterparts to term life insurance. Like term life, the policyholder pays an agreed annual premium and, when the insured dies, the amount of the death benefit is paid to the beneficiary. Built into these policies is the expense of an internal savings / investment account.

from estate taxes and may soon repeal them altogether. While there are special cases that would be an exception to this, once your net worth reaches critical mass, you can say goodbye to your life insurance policies.

TERM OR WHOLE LIFE?

Consumers have become much more savvy during the past twenty-five years. There was a time when everyone purchased whole life insurance without question. The idea behind whole life insurance is that your premium would be applied to both a death benefit (the amount your beneficiary receives upon your death) and a savings or investment account inside the policy as well.

151

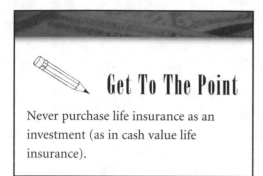

Get To The Point

Never purchase life insurance as an investment (as in cash value life insurance).

The drawbacks of combining investing with life insurance are numerous. The first is the significant increase in cost. Because this type of policy costs so much more, people cannot afford to purchase a large enough death benefit to protect their family. Secondly, the savings component of the policy is really a misnomer as the money withdrawn reduces the death benefit by an equal amount. What's even worse is that such withdrawals are treated as a loan that you must pay interest on. While some of the interest is actually paid back to your own account, interest must also be paid to the insurance company. You are in essence paying interest to borrow your own money! So what you have is very expensive life insurance coupled with a very ineffective savings mechanism. The most practical way to deal with the issue of investing and life insurance is to handle each separately.

The most cost-effective form of life insurance is term life insurance. Term life is now much more widely sold than whole life and represents a far greater amount of the total insurance in force today. "Term" simply

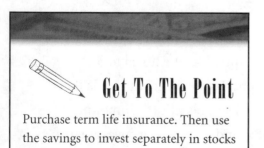

Get To The Point

Purchase term life insurance. Then use the savings to invest separately in stocks and mutual funds.

refers to the fact that you are covered for a specific term, usually one year, although you can lock in your rates for up to twenty years of coverage with a 100 percent guarantee that you can never be canceled. For example, I pay only about $80 per month for each one million dollars of term life insurance I buy.

What's more, this rate is locked in for another fifteen years. You, too, can take advantage of these kinds of rates. How much you pay will be determined by your age and medical history. The older you are and the more health problems you have, the more you will pay. I have shown people how to dump their whole life insurance and replace it with as much as ten times the term coverage for the same money! One warning about replacing life insurance: *Never cancel your existing policy until you have a new policy in force.* Your new policy may not be in force at the time you fill out the application.

In many cases you must wait for the policy to be delivered to you. In some circumstances the agent may be able to give you a "binder" which gives you temporary coverage until your policy is approved. In any case, do not cancel your current coverage until you receive your final approval and your policy is in hand.

Most of the quote services I have listed will provide you with a specific company's financial rating. If you want to check out a company on your own go to www.insure.com or www.ambest.com.

Money Talk

Annual renewable term life provides a guaranteed renewal without qualifying. *Level term* means that the annual premium amount can be locked in for five, ten, fifteen, or even twenty years.

HOW MUCH LIFE INSURANCE IS ENOUGH?

There are a number of methods commonly used to determine how much life insurance a person needs. These methods often include complicated calculations and worksheets. I won't burden you with that

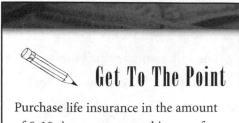

Get To The Point

Purchase life insurance in the amount of 8-10 times your annual income from companies with at least an A rating.

type of approach because the issue need not be overly complicated. A quick rule of thumb is to purchase between eight and ten times the income you are trying to replace. This means if you earn $40,000 each year, you would purchase between $320,000 and $400,000 in coverage (death benefit). This may sound like a lot of coverage, but it is the correct amount based on this income. The idea here is to determine how much money is required to replace 80 to 90 percent of your income. Consequently $400,000 invested (and earning 8 to 10 percent) would be the right amount.

Another simple approach breaks things down into two categories. The first issue is to make a list of all of your debts and determine what it would cost to pay off everything, leaving the family debt free. The second step would be to determine what amount of annual income would be required for the family to live comfortably after all family debts are paid off. You might determine that you need $200,000 to pay off the mortgage and all other debts (cars, credit cards, etc.). Next you conclude that, without the debt, the family could easily live on $25,000 per year. You would then work off a multiple of eight to ten times the $25,000.

In this example the following amount of life insurance would need to be purchased:

- $200,000 to pay off all family debt;
- $200,000-$250,000 for the generation of income.

This would bring the total amount of life insurance needed to $400,000-$450,000.

INSURING A STAY-AT-HOME PARENT

Although a parent who stays home with the children may not be earning any income, there is still a financial risk in the event of his or her death. Domestic and childcare services that previously had been provided out of love would now

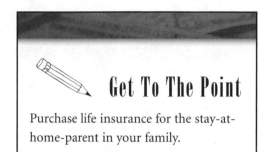

Get To The Point

Purchase life insurance for the stay-at-home-parent in your family.

have to be paid for. As children get older and reach their teenage years, this may become much less of a need. If you have children under the age of ten, you should consider purchasing a term life insurance policy in the amount of about ten times what it would cost to hire a domestic worker in your home. For example, if the average cost of hiring an individual to care for your children and home in your area is $20,000, you would need to purchase a $200,000 life insurance policy for the stay-at-home parent.

HEALTH INSURANCE

If you have employer-provided coverage, you can probably skip this section. If, on the other hand, you are among the forty million Americans who currently are without health insurance, read on.

Health or medical insurance is comprised of three major benefit areas:

- Outpatient services (doctors' visits, etc.);
- Inpatient services (hospital stays, surgery, emergency room services, etc.);
- Prescription drug benefits.

Within the world of health insurance, there are a variety of choices. Among them are:

- Health Maintenance Organizations (HMOs);
- Preferred Provider Organizations (PPOs).

The main difference between these two forms of coverage is that members of a PPO can more affordably use doctors outside the plan, while HMOs will cover little or nothing if you obtain medical services from outside their provider group. A third type of plan is known as "open choice," which allows you to choose your own doctor or hospital without restriction. However, these plans are becoming very rare and are usually prohibitively expensive. Your choice between an HMO or PPO may hinge more on which doctors are providing the services in your area than any other consideration. I personally have no preference between these two primary forms of coverage.

Money Talk

A *co-payment* is the amount of required out-of-pocket expense, usually a specific percentage or dollar amount. A *deductible* is the required dollar amount—at 100 percent of the cost—that must be paid before the insurance policy benefits kick in. The *stop loss provision* is the most that can be charged on a claim, usually for the year. (Some stop loss provision clauses are for different time periods. Check your policy for your specific coverage.)

As with many other types of insurance coverage, a simple method of lowering your costs is to partially self-insure. In the case of health insurance, the amount of money that you pay is comprised of the co-payment and the deductible. Most HMOs and PPOs have a set out-of-pocket amount required for doctor's visits and prescription drugs (which can vary anywhere from $5 to $30).

As an example, we'll look at a policy with a $1,000 deductible, an 80/20 co-payment, and a stop loss provision of $5,000. Under these policy provisions, $50,000 medical expenses within one year would cost the patient:

- $1,000 (the deductible);
- $4,000 (20 percent of the remaining $49,000 would be $9,800, but the stop loss limit is $5,000 and the $1000 deductible is included in the total).
- Total out-of-pocket expense is $5,000. The insurance company pays $45,000.

All health insurance policies have maximum policy limits (the most they will pay out over the life of the policy). The most typical maximum benefit is one million dollars. This may appear to be a significant amount, but anything less than that would not be prudent based on the current cost of medical services.

Now that I have covered the technicalities of health insurance, let's make things simple. Either you have employer-provided coverage or you don't. If you are not among the fortunate who receive health insurance as a part of your employment, you will have to go out and purchase it as an individual or as a small group if you are self-employed. This means that you may have to settle for less coverage. It also means that you might pay more since you are not a member of a large group.

SHOP FOR HEALTH INSURANCE ON THE INTERNET

The best Web site for health insurance shopping is www.ehealthinsurance.com. This site provides on-line shopping for both individual and group plans. They also offer a good overview that will help you understand the wide array of choices available.

Money Talk

What is *Cobra?* No, in this case it is not a snake or a fancy sports car. Cobra is a provision that allows you to continue to keep your health insurance coverage if you discontinue your employment. The good news is that you can keep your coverage for up to eighteen months. The bad news is that you must personally pay the entire cost.

Many people find it unaffordable to purchase the same kind of health insurance that is provided to the employees of major corporations. Again, going it alone makes the "blue chip" policies unaffordable for individual buyers. An often-overlooked alternative to buying a fully loaded health insurance plan with all of the extras is to settle for basic major medical coverage.

Major medical coverage will not cover the cost of prescription drugs or doctor's visits. The purpose of the coverage is to insure against catastrophic inpatient medical treatment. Although a variety of deductible and co-payments are available, the cost is very affordable when a high deductible like $5,000 is chosen. Yes, there is some risk for that amount of money, but it is far better than carrying no health insurance at all.

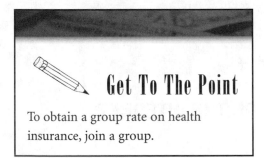

Get To The Point

To obtain a group rate on health insurance, join a group.

Gold Rule Insurance is one company that offers affordable major medical insurance. You can contact the company by calling (800) 444-8990 or by visiting their Web site, www.goldenrule.com.

Without a doubt, a consumer buying health insurance individually rather than as a part of a group is at a significant disadvantage. One way to beat this is to simply join a group. This may be simpler than you think. Most professional associations have group health insurance available to their members. If you are in a trade or just about any , you will find a selection of associations you can join. Go to your local library and ask your reference librarian for the *Directory of Associations.* This telephone-book-size directory will provide you with hundreds of opportunities to join a group.

What is the MIB? It is not "Men in Black" or any relation to the FBI, but it is equally as powerful in the world of insurance. Similar to a credit bureau, the Medical Information Bureau maintains a database of medical histories and must report to the Federal Trade Commission. If you have been turned down for insurance,

Money Talk

The MIB, *Medical Information Bureau,* keeps information on most Americans' medical records. Think of it as a sort of credit bureau on your health.

coverage it could be linked to a mistake in your file. For $8.50 you can obtain a copy of your file at their site, www.mib.com. Much like credit bureaus, you do have specific rights. Go through your file to see if there are any errors. If there are, make sure to provide corrections. The truth is out there.

INTERNET TIME SAVERS

Insurance Shopping and Research

www.tenday.com

www.myratesaver.com—Free insurance shopping service (most forms of coverage).

www.quotesmith.com—Auto, homeowner's, renter's, health, term life, dental, Medicare supplement, long-term care, disability, boat, watercraft, RV, motorcycle.

www.selectquote.com—Term life.

www.quotesusa.com—Auto, homeowner's, renter's, health, life, business.

www.insweb.com—Auto, homeowner's, renters, health, life, RVs, even pets.

www.accuquote.com—Life (rated 4 stars by *Consumer's Digest*).

www.quickquote.com—Auto, health, life, mortgage center, annuities.

www.ambest.com—Insurance company ratings.

www.ehealthinsurance.com—Health.

www.iiin.com—Insurance Industry Internet Network (a comprehensive network to all insurance-related issues).

FAST TRACK

1. It is an important part of your financial responsibility to make provision for you family in the event of a catastrophic medical expense, and especially in the event of a death.
2. You do not need to purchase every form of insurance that is available. Most people need life insurance, auto insurance, health insurance, homeowner's insurance, and personal liability.
3. Do not buy life insurance if you are a single person unless you have economic dependents.
4. Once your net worth reaches a point that you are financially independent, life insurance in no longer necessary.

5. The best form of life insurance is term life. Whole life and other formats are much more expensive and are not the best choice.

6. If you need to purchase your own health insurance, you should consider buying just major medical coverage. To make it more affordable, carry a higher deductible such as $2,500 or even $5,000.

7. Disability insurance is expensive and is often difficult to collect. If you do decide to purchase, ask for the policy to include a six-month "waiting period." This will bring down the cost, but means you will have to wait six months prior to receiving any benefits if you become disabled.

8. If possible, join a professional or trade group to get a "group rate" on health insurance.

9. Obtain a copy of your medical history from the Medical Information Bureau and update and correct it if necessary.

DAY 7 DIARY

I am on my way to my financial breakthrough. Today I . . .

_____

_____

_____

_____

_____

_____

_____

_____

_____

_____

_____

_____

_____

_____

_____

_____

_____

_____

Day 8

Investigate Your Insurance, Part 2

S	M	T	W	T	F	S
7		⑧	9	10		

✔ Now that you have reached day eight of your journey, we will focus on completing the task of creating your comprehensive insurance plan. We will discuss auto, homcowner's, and liability insurance as you finalize your overall insurance strategy. As promised, here are the passwords for access to www.tenday.com. Username: breakthrough. Password: mytenday. Both must be typed in all lowercase letters.

WHAT YOU WILL NEED:

- Auto, homeowner's, and liability policies.
- Insurance policy list from Day 7.

Cashing In

The amount you can save on auto and homeowner's insurance will depend on your specific circumstances, but comparable plans can vary widely in price from company to company. It is very possible that you could save $250 or more per year on these policies. $250 invested at 11 percent for 25 years can grow to $28,600. Hey, all of this money is really starting to add up isn't it? Another benefit is that your total insurance protection should increase as well. While it may not have a specific dollar value, in the event of a catastrophic situation, this advantage could be priceless.

Get To The Point

Carry higher deductibles for substantial discounts.

AUTOMOBILE INSURANCE

If you drive a vehicle, purchasing auto insurance is not an option. To my knowledge, every state in America requires some minimum amount of coverage if you are going to operate a motor vehicle. The questions we do need to ask are: How much insurance do you need? And how do you find the best price?

Auto insurance coverage is broken down into three major components:

·   *Collision*—Covers damage to your automobile in the event of an accident.
·   *Comprehensive*—Covers damage to your automobile from perils such as vandalism, fire, and other "non-moving" catastrophes.
·   *Liability*—Covers damage to other people and their property (this will be listed on your policy as bodily injury liability and property damage liability).

One easy method of reducing your auto insurance premiums is to raise your deductible. Many insurance companies will offer you a 25 percent discount if you agree to a $500 deductible. You can get as much as a 50 percent discount if you carry a $1,000 deductible. The deductible is the amount of money you would have to pay in the event of a claim prior to the insurance picking up the difference. This means that if you are in an accident, you pay the first $500.

Carrying higher deductibles can save so much money that you can easily create an emergency savings account to cover your needs in the event of a car accident. This concept of carrying higher deductibles is actually a combination of *risk retention* and *risk transfer*. What we are doing is transferring the large risk (damages exceeding $500 or $1,000) to the insurance company, and retaining the smaller risk (damages less than this amount). This provides you with minimal risk and maximum savings.

Although car insurance policy perks such as free towing may not seem to be that expensive, add on too many of these "extras" and the cost of your policy goes up quickly. You can often obtain these extra benefits through less-expensive alternatives. One approach is to join AAA for all

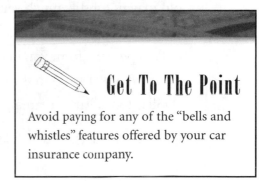

Get To The Point

Avoid paying for any of the "bells and whistles" features offered by your car insurance company.

of your roadside assistance needs and remove the cost of them from your auto insurance.

Although many insurance companies are joining the ranks of those that will quote auto insurance rates over the Internet, the best comprehensive site I have found is Quotesmith (www.quotesmith.com). Quotesmith will allow you to comparison-shop dozens of companies for the best auto insurance rates. You can find other on-line quote services by using any of the major search engines and typing in "on-line auto insurance quotes."

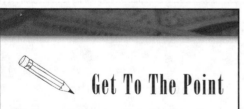

Money Talk

The *collision* and *comprehensive* elements of your insurance policy cover damage to *your* vehicle, while *liability* covers damage that you may cause to others and their property.

The collision and comprehensive elements of your auto insurance plan cover damage to your vehicle. The insurance company has the option of repairing your vehicle, replacing your vehicle, or paying you for the damage. This leaves you as a consumer in a position of not being able to collect more than the "book value" of your car. Vehicles with high mileage or more than five years old may not justify much value in an insurance claim. What this means is that while the insurance company will gladly accept hundreds of dollars per year from you in collision and comprehensive premiums, they will only pay up to the maximum of the vehicle's book value. (Dollar for dollar, you are paying in far more than you would receive.)

If your vehicle is worth less than $3,000, the best solution is "self-insurance" for this form of financial risk. Remember that self-insurance means you establish an emergency reserve account from your reduced insurance premiums. This account would be tapped into if you ever needed to make a repair to or completely replace your vehicle. Regardless of the value of your vehicle, you must always carry *liability coverage*.

Get To The Point

Remove collision and comprehensive coverage from your auto insurance policy if the value of your vehicle drops below $3,000.

Law requires this coverage. No matter how old your vehicle is, there is still the big risk of damaging other people or their property.

Although phone shopping and using the Internet will narrow your search for the best deal, you are not quite done. Be sure to ask about available discount plans being offered by the carriers on your short list. Some companies offer discounts for seniors, while others provide substantial savings when you purchase more than one policy from them. In other examples, there may be additional rate reductions for a good driving record or if you are a low-mileage driver. You most likely will not be offered these discounts unless you ask about them, so by all means do so.

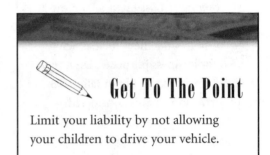

Get To The Point

Limit your liability by not allowing your children to drive your vehicle.

A frequent question I hear at seminars is about the whole matter of teenage drivers. There are a number of ways that this issue can be approached. Most parents opt to add their teenagers to the family insurance plan and give them access to the family vehicles. This can sometimes be done inexpensively if you can establish that the teenager is a "part-time" driver and if they have good grades (and minimal traffic tickets). The problem with your teenagers driving the family station wagon is the potential for a lawsuit. In most states, the driver *and* the owner of a vehicle can both be held

Money Talk

Lawyers often sue both the driver and the owner of a vehicle that is the cause of an accident. *Vicarious liability* means that you are responsible if you are the owner of the vehicle, even if you are not the driver during the accident.

responsible for damages resulting from an accident. My suggestion has always been to purchase an older model car to be shared by the teenagers in your household. The title to this car should be in the name of one or more of your teenage drivers. This will cost more from an insurance standpoint, but will keep you one step removed from any potential litigation. This approach is more affordable if you purchase an older vehicle and do not carry collision and comprehensive coverage.

Most auto insurance polices expressly do not cover commercial use. Even something as seemingly harmless as a teenager using the family car to deliver pizza at his after school job, would be deemed a "commercial use of the vehicle." This means that regardless of the amount of insurance you have in force, you may be without coverage during these times.

Money Talk

The *commercial use exclusion* on most auto policies means that you will not be covered while the vehicle is being used for business purposes. Driving to and from work would not fall under this exclusion (that is considered *commuting),* but performing tasks for your employer or making deliveries may be considered commercial use. Find out what your policy does and does not cover if you have any doubts.

Money Talk

Homeowner's insurance comes in many forms. If you own a house or condo, or even rent an apartment, there is a plan to cover your insurance needs.

HOMEOWNER'S INSURANCE

Homeowner's insurance is very similar to auto insurance: Liability covers you in the event that someone is injured while on your property or other incidents of personal liability away from your property and, secondly, damage to your property (i.e. fire, theft, burglary, tornado). Depending on where you live, you may need to purchase a number of policies to supplement your basic homeowner's plan. These polices might include flood insurance, wind insurance, and even earthquake insurance. In this chapter I will be addressing the issue of the basic homeowner's plan. If the area where you live is prone to additional perils, I highly encourage you to weigh the benefits of these other types of policies. For example, since I live near the Atlantic Ocean, my primary homeowner's policy specifically excludes wind damage. Consequently, I have had to purchase a separate policy to insure against this peril. Again, it is important that you do not purchase duplicate coverage.

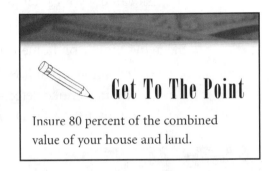

Get To The Point

Insure 80 percent of the combined value of your house and land.

One of the primary rules of property insurance is that you cannot collect for more than your actual damages. Consequently it makes no sense to purchase coverage that exceeds the value of your home. A rule of thumb that can be used is to purchase coverage in the amount of 80 percent of the combined value of your home and land. Even if your home is leveled, the land is still there. If you purchase a home for $100,000 you may only need $80,000 in coverage. A better, more precise way,

Money Talk

Guaranteed replacement coverage means that the insurance company agrees to rebuild or repair your home regardless of the cost to do so. The type of coverage is more expensive, but relieves you of having to make the determination of the insurable value of the property.

to approach this is to purchase "guaranteed replacement coverage." This will usually involve your insurance agent doing a complete analysis of the value of your home since the insurance company will now be responsible to completely rebuild your home in the event of a total loss.

As mentioned during day seven, self-insuring for a small amount of the risk can cut your premiums significantly. Expect discounts of 25 percent or more just for carrying higher deductibles. Additional means of saving money on homeowner's insurance may include:

- Installing a monitored alarm system.
- Adding smoke detectors and dead-bolt locks.
- Living near a fire station.

Get To The Point

Be sure to cover all personal property.

The matter of insuring personal property within a home is a tricky one. First of all, you must determine the value of what you have. Most people have no idea what the collective value is of all of their earthly possessions accumulated over the course of a lifetime. Although it may be challenging, you must come up with a figure. You will not collect any more than the *actual value* of your property, so it makes no sense to overstate here. On the other hand, you will not be able to collect more than the amount of insurance you purchase. The easiest way to approach this is to divide your personal belongings into two categories. First, those items that individually are valued at more than $3,000 and secondly those that are below this amount.

The higher value items may need to be specifically added to your policy on a special schedule. "Scheduling" higher priced items will greatly increase your chances of collecting their value in the event of a loss.

Another approach with higher priced items is to purchase a "floater policy." This type of policy will provide greater protection and make it much easier for you to collect. It is a good idea to have some basis of establishing value for your higher priced items. Whether you have a purchase receipt or an appraisal, it may come down to that piece of paper whether or not you collect. These types of documents should always be stored somewhere away from your property in case of a catastrophic event.

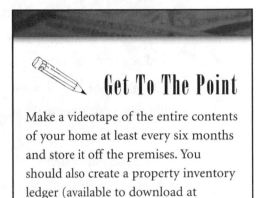

Get To The Point

Make a videotape of the entire contents of your home at least every six months and store it off the premises. You should also create a property inventory ledger (available to download at www.tenday.com).

After you have established the value of your items, you should have a good idea of the overall value of the contents in your home. It is an absolute must that you videotape the contents of your home at least every six months and store this tape away from your home. I suggest that you just do a simple walk through of your home with a video camera, and make sure you take at least 30-45 minutes to do a thorough job. You may also add simple commentary as you describe some of the items you are video taping. After completing your videotape, it is also a wise strategy to create an inventory ledger of your personal property as well. The video and the inventory ledger will create a permanent record in the event your home is burglarized or destroyed by fire or weather.

PERSONAL LIABILITY

A second critical element to your homeowner's insurance is liability. This has nothing to do with damage to your property or the loss of your belongings, but everything to do with people being injured while on your premises. These kinds of accidents can come as a complete surprise. (I guess the term "accident" is, by definition, a surprise. But you know what I mean.) People have shared the most unusual stories—everything from a simple tripping accident, to a lawn mower firing a rock at an individual walking by. Although legally it must be established that you were negligent, that doesn't take much in today's litigation-filled society. Most homeowner's policies carry maximum liability coverage of $100,000. That figure is not nearly enough, which is why I suggest a comprehensive personal liability plan known as an "umbrella liability" policy.

The liability portion of your homeowner's plan will also cover *personal liability* that you may incur while away from your home. Let's say that you accidentally break a neighbor's window while throwing a ball from down the street or drop an antique item while shopping. These incidents of personal liability may be covered even though you are not "home" when they occur.

I recommend that you carry a minimum of one million dollars in personal liability coverage. The best way to approach this is as follows: Contact the insurance company where your homeowner's and auto insurance policies are and obtain a quote on a one million dollar umbrella policy. Next, ask them what minimum liability coverage is

---

Money Talk

A *comprehensive personal liability policy* (sometimes called *umbrella liability*) provides coverage for matters of personal liability, regardless of where they occur. This type of policy will increase your liability coverage on both your auto and homeowner's plan. In addition to that, it will cover any matters of personal liability you may have even while away from your property or vehicle. Keep in mind that professional liability is not covered.

required on your auto and homeowner's policies in order for you to qualify for the umbrella plan. The way this works is that the one million-dollar liability policy will pick up if your auto or homeowner's liability runs out. For example, if you

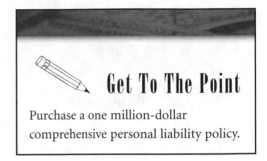

Get To The Point

Purchase a one million-dollar comprehensive personal liability policy.

were sued as a result of an accident at your home and the judgment was for one million dollars, you would be adequately insured. Even if you only had $100,000 of liability coverage on your homeowner's plan, the personal liability policy would pay the difference up to an additional one million dollars. The same would occur in an auto accident.

The great thing about a personal liability policy is that it covers virtually all matters of personal liability. This means that accidents that occur away from your home or when you are not driving would be covered. In many cases, by lowering your liability coverage on your auto and homeowner's plans, you can buy the umbrella coverage with the savings and end up with more insurance for less money! You can expect the first one million to cost you about $200-$250 per year and less for each million after that! I would suggest carrying more than one million if you have a high net worth.

You will find the Internet less of a resource in the category of homeowner's insurance than for other forms of insurance. Consequently, I would suggest that you talk with family and friends and find out how much they are paying and who their carrier is. Also, as mentioned earlier, I would consider purchasing your homeowner's plan from the same company as your auto insurance. This will open the door to additional discount opportunities.

Money Talk

If you are a renter you should purchase *contents only* insurance. Although you do not own your residence, you still can insure against the loss of your personal property. The building itself and other issues of liability are generally covered by the *owner* unless otherwise indicated in your lease.

RENTER'S INSURANCE

If you rent your home, condo, or apartment you still need *homeowner's insurance.* This form of homeowner's insurance is specifically designed for renters. The coverage is usually referred to as "contents only." What you are doing here is simply insuring against the loss of the contents within your rented dwelling. The individual you are renting from will already carry coverage for liability and damage to the building (unless otherwise indicated in your lease).

INTERNET TIME SAVERS

Insurance Shopping and Research

www.tenday.com

www.myratesaver.com—Free insurance shopping service (most forms of coverage).

www.quotesmith.com—Auto, homeowner's, renter's, health, term life, dental, Medicare supplement, long-term care, disability, boat, watercraft, RV, motorcycle.

www.selectquote.com—Term life.

www.quotesusa.com—Auto, homeowner's, renter's, health, life, business.

www.insweb.com—Auto, homeowner's, renters, health, life, RVs, even pets.

www.accuquote.com—Life (rated 4 stars by Consumer's Digest).

www.quickquote.com—Auto, health, life, mortgage center, annuities.

www.ambest.com—Insurance company ratings.

www.ehealthinsurance.com—Health.

www.iiin.com—Insurance Industry Internet Network (a comprehensive network to all insurance-related issues).

FAST TRACK

1. Auto insurance is comprised of two elements:
   1) *Collision/comprehensive* covers damage to your vehicle;
   2) *Liability* provides protection against damage to other people and their property.
2. Carry a $500 deductible and expect up to a 25 percent discount. Ask for a $1,000 deductible and save up to 50 percent!
3. Most "bells and whistles" extras are not worth the money. Skip the optional perks like towing, roadside assistance, etc. and join AAA instead.
4. Use the Internet to shop for the best auto insurance rates.
5. If the value of your vehicle is less than $3,000, drop the collision and comprehensive coverage. You can only collect on the book value of your car. Why pay expensive premiums for such a small amount of potential recovery ($3,000 or less)?
6. Ask about auto insurance discount plans. If you purchase your homeowner's and auto plan from the same company, have a good driving record, are a senior citizen, are a low-mileage driver, or have a safe driving record, you may be eligible for big

discounts. Ask about discounts, as they may not be offered to you otherwise.

7. Most auto insurance plans do not cover commercial use. Do not use your vehicle for business purposes unless you also purchase commercial insurance.

8. As the owner of a vehicle you can be held legally responsible if another person driving your car is involved in an accident. The best plan for teenage drivers is to help them purchase their own used car so you cannot be sued if they are in an accident.

9. Homeowner's insurance has both a property element and a liability element. Be sure that your home is insured completely. Determine the cost of replacing your home and the value of your personal property.

10. Some homeowners opt for guaranteed replacement coverage. It is more expensive, but guarantees that your home would be rebuilt regardless of cost.

11. Any individual items valued at $3,000 or more should be individually itemized on your policy or "scheduled."

12. Make a video of the interior of your home and its contents every six months. It is also wise to compile an inventory ledger of your personal property. Both the ledger and the video should, of course, be stored away from your home. You can download a personal property inventory template at www.tenday.com.

13. Purchase at least one million dollars of personal liability coverage. This type of policy will pick up where your auto and homeowner's insurance end. These policies normally cost about $200 to $250 per year.

14. If you are a renter, you need "contents coverage." This means that you are insuring against only the loss of your personal property and not the building (since you landlord would normally do that).

DAY 8 DIARY

I am on my way to my financial breakthrough. Today I . . .

_____

_____

_____

_____

_____

_____

_____

_____

_____

_____

_____

_____

_____

_____

_____

_____

_____

_____

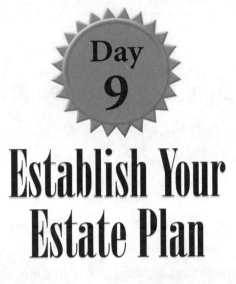

Day 9

Establish Your Estate Plan

S	M	T	W	T	F	S
7	8	⑨	10			

✔ This is day nine of your breakthrough, and you are only two days from the finish line! Today you will learn why everyone needs a will, how to prepare your own will, how to reduce your estate tax burden, and determine whether or not a trust is a necessity for your family.

WHAT YOU WILL NEED:

- The name of your choice for guardian of your minor children in the event of your death.
- A list of who you want to receive your assets upon your death.
- The current value of your estate.

CHRISTIAN MONEY PRINCIPLE

Providing for your family after your death is a significant part of Christian stewardship. *A good man leaves an inheritance for his children's children* (Proverbs 13:22).

What part does creating a plan for death play in a financial strategy for life? I don't know if any of us ever really become comfortable with the issue of death. But as troubling as it is to think about, it will happen to us all. No one knows if they have thirty years or thirty minutes left on this earth. There are no guarantees, and no one knows the future.

Cashing In

Dying without a proper estate plan can cost your family tens of thousands of dollars in legal fees and can potentially cause years of delay until your estate is settled. Those who own family businesses, farms, or other high-net worth assets face the risk of losing as much as half of their estate through federal and state estate taxes. By taking a few simple steps such as creating a will or, even better a living trust, you can reduce, or completely eliminate your estate taxes.

Consequently, we may sit down and pound out the numbers—making assumptions about saving a certain amount each month for twenty or thirty years or even longer—even though it is uncertain whether we will even live another day. How then do we incorporate the fact that we do not know when we will die into our financial planning? One large element of this is proper planning with life insurance.

As we have already discussed, if we die prior to accumulating enough money for our family's future, the right amount of life insurance will kick in and make up the balance. That is important, but there are even more complicated issues than buying the right dollar amount of insurance. These issues involve the legal quagmire of transferring assets from the dead to the living. There have been stories of celebrities' estates that were tied up for nearly twenty years. Although it is unlikely your estate will face problems of this magnitude (unless you are a movie star or extremely wealthy), even a delay of two to three years can be financially devastating to your family.

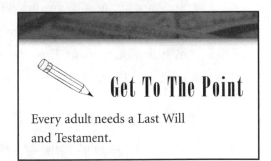

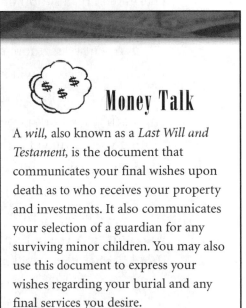

Get To The Point

Every adult needs a Last Will and Testament.

WHY IS A WILL ESSENTIAL?

I meet thousands of people each year who readily admit to not having a will. Although the statistics vary widely, it is believed that more than 70 percent of Americans do not have a valid will. Why is this a problem? A person who dies without a will dies "intestate." This means that state law will determine who receives the assets, and a state judge will determine who becomes the guardian of any minor children. The most pressing issue in my opinion, *much* more than money, is that of guardianship. If something were to happen to you, would you want a judge who knows nothing about you

Money Talk

A *will*, also known as a *Last Will and Testament*, is the document that communicates your final wishes upon death as to who receives your property and investments. It also communicates your selection of a guardian for any surviving minor children. You may also use this document to express your wishes regarding your burial and any final services you desire.

or your family deciding who should raise your children? This situation alone should be sufficient motivation for taking the time to write a will.

Creating a valid will is one of *the most important steps* you can take in your financial planning. I believe that the finality of death is something that requires significant attention on the part of any responsible person. It is your last act of stewardship to transfer your assets to those you determine should receive them.

WHERE TO BEGIN

Traditionally, wills are prepared by attorneys. If you are married, both you and your spouse each need a separate will document. Most married couples simply leave everything to the surviving spouse upon their death. In the unlikely event of their simultaneous deaths, they would leave their estate to their children and appoint a guardian for them. If you are a single person, you may decide to leave your estate to a charitable organization or to your parents. You can list any person(s) or organization(s) that you would like to receive your money.

In recent years, more people have created a will on their own. You will find a variety of will kits available at your local office supply or bookstore. If you have a very simple situation, the "do it yourself approach" may work perfectly fine for you. The only problem with writing your own will is that if you make a mistake or are inadvertently ambiguous, you cannot come back from the dead to deal with the error. Following is a sample will template that you may wish to use. However, you should always have any will you prepare on your own reviewed by your attorney. The bottom line is that everyone reading this book should either have a will drawn up by an attorney, or create a self-prepared will at the very least. The following document can be downloaded at www.tenday.com.

LAST WILL AND TESTAMENT OF

[Your name]

I, [**Insert your name**], of [**Insert your address**], being of sound and disposing mind, do hereby make, publish, and declare the following to be my Last Will and Testament, revoking all previous will and codicils made by me.

I declare that I am married to [**Insert your spouse's name**], to which I have referred to herein as my "spouse," and that I have [**Insert number of children**] children now living whose names and birth dates are: [**List children's full names and birth dates**].

I have [**Insert number**] deceased children.

All references to "my children" in this will include all of the above-named children and also any child hereafter born or adopted by me.

I.   My spouse and I are executing wills at approximately the same time in which each is the primary beneficiary of the other. These wills are not being made because of any contractual agreement between us, and either will may at any time be revoked by either maker at the sole discretion thereof.

II.   I appoint my spouse as personal representative of my will. If unable or unwilling to act, or to continue to act, as executor of my will, I then appoint [**Insert your successor personal representative**] as personal representative of my will.

No bond or other security of any kind shall be required of any personal representative appointed in this will.

My personal representative, whether original, substitute, or successor, shall hereafter also be referred to as my "executor."

III. I direct that my executor pay all of my funeral expenses, all state and federal estate, inheritance, and succession taxes, administration costs, and all of my debts subject to statute of limitations, except mortgage notes secured by real estate, as soon as practical.

IV.   I give, devise, and bequeath all of the rest, residue, and remainder of my estate, of whatever kind and character, and wherever located, to my spouse, provided that my spouse survives me.

I make no provision for my children, knowing that, as their parent, my spouse will continue to be mindful of their needs and requirements.

V.   If my spouse does not survive me, then I give, devise, and bequeath all of the rest, residue, and remainder of my estate, of whatever kind and character, and wherever located, to my children per stirpes, and I direct that the share of any child of mine who shall have died leaving no issue shall be divided among my surviving children in equal shares per stirpes.

VI.   My executor shall have the following additional powers with respect to my estate, to be exercised from time to time at my executor's discretion without further license or order of any court.

BUSINESS INTEREST

To sell or otherwise liquidate, or to continue to operate at my executor's discretion, any corporation, partnership or other business interest received by my estate.

PROPERTY OF MY ESTATE

To retain any and all property and securities of my estate in the name of my executor as executor or in my executor's own name.

RETENTION OF ASSETS

To retain all property and securities of my estate for as long as my executor deems advisable.

MANAGEMENT OF ESTATE

To invest, lease, rent, mortgage, insure, repair, improve, or sell any and all real and personal property belonging to my estate, as my executor deems advisable.

MORTGAGES, PLEDGES, AND DEEDS OF TRUST

To enforce any and all mortgages, pledges, and deeds of trust held by my estate and to purchase at any sale thereunder any such real or personal property subject to any mortgage, pledge, or deed of trust.

LITIGATION

To initiate or defend, at my executor's discretion, any litigation affecting my estate.

ATTORNEYS, ADVISORS, AND AGENTS

To employ and to pay from my estate reasonable compensation to such attorneys, accountants, brokers, and investment, tax and other advisors as my executor shall deem advisable.

ADJUSTMENT OF CLAIMS

To submit to arbitration, to compromise or to release or otherwise adjust, with or without compensation, any and all claims affecting the trust estate.

DISTRIBUTION OF MY ESTATE

In distributing my estate, to make said distribution wholly or partly in kind by transferring or allotting such real or personal property or undivided interest therein.

VII. If any person, whether or not related to me by blood or in any way, shall attempt, either directly or indirectly, to set aside the probate of my will or oppose any of the provisions hereof, and such person shall establish a right to any portion of my estate, then I give and bequeath the sum of one dollar ($1.00), only that, and no further interest whatever in my estate to such person.

VIII. In the event that any of my property, or all of it, at the time of my death is community property under the laws of any jurisdiction, then my will shall be construed as referring only to my community-property interest therein.

IX. If any portion of my will shall be held illegal, invalid, or otherwise inoperative, it is my intention that all of the other provisions hereof shall continue to be fully effective and operative insofar as is possible and reasonable.

IN WITNESS WHEREOF, I have hereto set my hand and seal this _____ day of _____, 20___.

_____ **(Insert Notary Signature)**

WITNESS NAMES AND SIGNATURES   WITNESS ADDRESS

_____   _____

Name:

_____   _____

Name:

After your attorney has reviewed your will, you should have it notarized and witnessed by no fewer than two individuals.

I recommend that you choose witnesses who are disinterested parties. For example, if the two witnesses are the two children receiving the bulk of your estate, it could leave an opening for a fraud argument by any other children who are receiving less. Since the document will be longer than one page, you should also initial each page in the lower right-hand corner. You should have your witnesses initial as well. This will prevent any potential claim that any of the pages have been modified. I would execute at least two originals. One original can be kept in your home and the second in a safe deposit box or other location that is outside your home.

You should always make the location of your documents known to at least one individual that does not live with you. Many people ask their attorney or financial planner to keep an original of the document in their office. This is up to you. Your state's laws may limit whom you choose to act as your personal representative (what is sometimes called an executor). In some jurisdictions, this person must also be a resident of your county or state. Be sure to check your local laws prior to making this decision. You may also name a second choice for your personal representative if, for some reason, your first choice is not willing or able to perform the assigned duties.

If you change addresses, get married or divorced, or experience any other material change in your financial status, update your will as soon as possible. I meet with clients

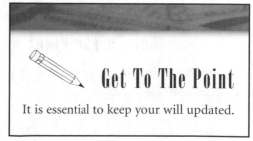

Get To The Point

It is essential to keep your will updated.

who have not modified their wills in more than ten years. Don't let that describe your situation! People like this may now have children who are legal adults, they may have moved, their financial status may have completely changed, and the will document has become almost worthless as a result. You might want to store your will document on a word processor and make changes when necessary. Of course, you must always destroy all previous wills and have the new will notarized and witnessed all over again.

Money Talk

Probate is a public legal process which involves reviewing a will to be sure that it is valid.

Probate is the legal process that your estate will go through even if you have a will. There is a common misconception that wills are not subject to probate. Even though you have taken the step to write a will, it will still have to go through the process known as probate. There is only one way to avoid probate: Create a living trust (more on that later).

Probate is the process that involves reviewing the will to be sure that it is valid. Any questions about the validity of the document will be litigated at this time. This is the stage where forgotten relatives may show up on the scene to demand their "fair share," etc. It is also the time for creditors to make their claim on the assets of the estate.

Get To The Point

Probate takes time, is a public process, and can consume a considerable amount of your estate (5 to 15 percent).

There is usually a requirement for a public advertisement of the probate and notice given to all potential creditors to come forward. In Florida a ninety-day waiting period follows this advertisement. After ninety days have passed, the process of settling the estate may begin. It may not happen quickly, however. If there are assets that cannot readily be turned into cash (such as real estate), the will may stipulate that these items be sold. In these cases, it is conceivable that the process could easily take longer than a year. The process could be further delayed if any disputes arise with creditors making a claim or with individuals contesting the will. In addition, up to 15 percent of the entire estate may be spent on the legal fees for getting all of this done. On top of the delay and the cost, imagine everyone in your town knowing everything about your estate and who is getting what. This will happen because probate is a very public process and has no concern for the privacy of a family.

In any case, matters are far more difficult if you don't have a will. Don't for a minute make a decision not to make a will because of my description of probate. If you want to avoid probate, I will teach you how to do that in the following pages by establishing a living trust.

MAKING CHANGES TO A WILL

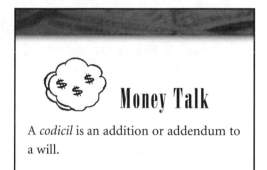

Money Talk

A *codicil* is an addition or addendum to a will.

Many people make additions to their will through what is know as a codicil. I am not an advocate of codicils as I find them to be confusing to understand when used in addition to the original will document. In my opinion, it is worth the extra time and effort to rewrite your will and not use codicils. After the will is written, if you make changes orally to your loved ones, don't expect that to be legally enforceable.

DISINHERITING

I often receive questions about how to *not* include certain individuals in a will. If you have a child or other family member who is financially irresponsible, or for some other reason you do not want to include in the will, you have that option. Attorneys usually suggest special declaratory language if you are leaving a close family member out of your will. For example, you might write "I am not leaving any money to my son Jim since he is an author and financial planner and has more than enough money of his own." If you have a relative that you suspect might cause trouble with your estate, you should definitely meet with an attorney to discuss it. The best way to deal with the issue is to mention that person by name in your will and state that you are not leaving them anything. This dispels any claim that you may have "accidentally left them out of the will."

In most states you cannot disinherit your spouse. Even if you were to write your will with specific instructions to leave your spouse none of your assets, there are usually statutory minimums that your spouse will receive. If you have been married more than once, this brings in the additional complication of what rights a former spouse may have to your estate. These issues are generally dealt with when a divorce is finalized, but don't count on that. If you have been divorced, you should definitely work out your will with an attorney. If you have children from a prior marriage, there could be a substantial court battle over your current spouse's rights versus those of your minor children and/or former spouse.

PRENUPTIAL AGREEMENTS

I am not an advocate of prenuptial agreements, but they do have their place in certain situations. If you have been married before and have children from a prior marriage, you may need to have your current spouse agree to your intentions to leave certain assets to your children. In other cases, if you own a family

Money Talk

A *prenuptial agreement* is a legal document drawn up prior to a marriage that spells out how assets are to be distributed in the event of a divorce.

business you may have the intention of leaving the business to a family member other than your spouse. In these cases, and others, a prenuptial agreement is probably the only legally binding way to limit your spouse from overriding your written will document upon your death.

If you are pursuing a prenuptial agreement exclusively as a way of keeping your finances separate from your spouse's, I recommend you reconsider. The biblical philosophy of "two becoming one" is in direct contradiction with that. I have learned, however, that it is naïve to suggest that prenuptial agreements should not be considered under *any* circumstances. Even with Christian couples who have very honorable intentions, there are dozens of very good reasons to employ the use of a prenuptial document. Of course, the best strategy is to meet with your attorney on these issues.

WHAT IS A TRUST?

A trust, like a will, is just a piece of paper. What it does is very powerful, however. The laws of your state dictate that once a person dies his or her assets must go through a special review process. These laws do not apply to assets that are owned by a trust. Consequently, your family can enjoy immediate and uninterrupted access to your investments and other assets if you take the simple step of writing a trust with your attorney.

Money Talk

A *living trust document* is used for the purpose of transferring ownership of your assets from your name into the name of a trust. This is done to avoid probate and can also be combined with other trust strategies to reduce or eliminate estate taxes.

It is a common misconception that trusts are only for the rich. There are various types of trusts, but consistent with the theme of this book, I am just going to deal with the basics. I will focus on the issue of an "intervivos" trust, otherwise known as a living trust. The living trust document provides three primary benefits:

- Avoids probate (and conservatorship if you become incapacitated).
- Complete privacy of your estate after your death.
- Can be a part of an overall strategy to reduce your estate taxes.

The idea behind a living trust is a fairly simple one. The process involves creating a legal entity. This is really no different from forming a corporation, limited partnership, or other legal structure. Once you have formed the trust, you then fund it. Funding occurs when you transfer ownership of your property to the name of the trust. This is a very simple process that banks and brokerage firms deal with every day, so you will not face any difficulty changing the title of your assets to reflect that they are owned by the trust.

Upon your death, any property not titled in the name of the trust will go through probate. The only exception to this rule is an asset that is allowed by law to skip the probate process. These are assets that allow for a beneficiary designation such as IRA accounts, retirement plans, annuities, and life insurance proceeds. Addressing this exception is as simple as naming your trust as the beneficiary of these types of assets. This, too, is a very common process. Call your broker, insurance agent, or banker and ask for a change of beneficiary form and list your trust.

The legal concept behind the trust is that when you die, your property is now entirely owned by the trust and the trust lives on even after your death. It is nothing more complicated than that. Although it is a simple strategy, it is a very powerful one.

WHAT ARE ESTATE TAXES?

You pay taxes when you earn money, spend it, or invest it; and what is left may be taxed again. You may be subject to estate taxes on both the state level and the federal level. I will leave up to you the project of learning about your state estate tax provisions, as each state is unique in this regard. Some states do not tax estates at all, while others seem to have gone crazy with the amount of taxes they require. The most you can pay on the federal level is 55 percent, which is based on a sliding scale.

The federal government and most state governments provide a base amount that your estate can be worth without being subject to any estate taxes (estate tax exclusion). A critical issue is to understand what comprises the value of your estate. Most people find it hard to believe that their estate is worth millions of dollars, but it is not as uncommon as you might imagine. Your estate value includes all of your real estate, securities investments, all personal property, the value of any businesses you own, and any life insurance proceeds if you were the insurance policy owner. Although life insurance proceeds are not subject to income taxes, they may be subject to estate taxation. One way to avoid this tax is to set up a life insurance trust. The trust must be set up at least three years prior to your death. You can then make gifts to the trust each year to cover the premiums. I will not go into this any further in this book other than to let you know that this strategy can be employed, and any trained financial planner or attorney can give you more details.

SAVING MONEY ON ESTATE TAXES WITH A LIVING TRUST

A living trust alone will not save you money on estate taxes. This is a common myth. If you are a married person, you can leave an unlimited amount of assets to your spouse without any estate tax liability. The problem of estate taxes occurs on the death of the second spouse. At the time of writing this book, the matter of federal estate taxation is in a great deal of flux. We are currently on a sliding increase of the estate tax exclusion.

Most American families will not owe estate taxes since the newly enacted law raises the current $675, 000 per-person exemption to $1 million in 2002 and eventually to $3.5 million in 2009. The problem with these figures is that they are likely to keep changing. What is even more confusing is that the segments of the current legislation must be renewed by a future Congress in 2010 or they will "sunset" (political language for automatic disappearance). So what is a person to do? If your estate is currently greater than $1,000,000 you might consider combining a living trust with a credit shelter trust.

ESTATE TAXES EXEMPTION

2002-03:	1 million
2004-05:	1.5 million
2006-08:	2 million
2009:	3.5 million
2010:	complete repeal

Money Talk

A credit shelter trust can be used to allow each marital partner to enjoy the current maximum exclusion from estate taxes. This means that in 2002 and after (barring future tax code changes) a married couple could shelter up to two million dollars from estate taxes (and more as the

Money Talk

A *credit shelter trust* document is used by attorneys for the purpose of doubling the estate tax exemption for married couples (giving each spouse an exemption, rather than having one exemption apply to both). This strategy is applied only to couples, as singles cannot increase their exemption amount.

exemption increases). The trust provides that upon the death of the first spouse, two trusts are formed. Many times this is called an "A-B trust" which describes the formation of the two trusts that comprise the strategy. I will not go into this any further other than to let you know about it. If you have an estate greater than two million dollars, it would be beneficial to discuss this type of trust with your lawyer.

WRITING YOUR OWN TRUST

While it is possible to obtain the documents to create a trust on your own, I strongly recommend that you use a professional once you reach the point of moving beyond a basic will. A living trust/credit shelter combination will cost between $700 and $1,000 in most states. If you throw in a life insurance trust, you may spend an additional $300.

You can determine the size of your estate by taking your net worth figure from day one and adding any life insurance death benefits. This will give you a basis for determining whether you are a candidate for a trust or not.

INTERNET TIME SAVERS

Estate Planning Resources

www.tenday.com—Features a free online will kit.

www.nolo.com—Nolo Press. A great site loaded with legal resources and an informative section on wills and trusts.

www.lawinfo.com—Probably one of the largest legal resource sites on the Internet. Of course, they have a wide variety of tools and information on estate planning.

www.attorneyfind.com—If you are looking for an attorney, you can find one in about thirty seconds using this resource. Users select their geographical location and the legal specialty they are seeking.

www.legalopinion.com—Provides a legal opinion for $35 and offers a free attorney referral service.

www.lawyers.com—Not simply a large resource of legal information, but the largest directory of lawyers on or off the Internet.

FAST TRACK

1. A will determines who will receive your property upon your death. Your will also appoints a guardian for your minor children.
2. Every adult needs a basic will.
3. You can create your own will or use a will kit. A free basic will template is available at www.tenday.com.
4. Although you can create your own will, the best option is to utilize an attorney.
5. Your will must be updated as your financial circumstances change.
6. A codicil is an addition to a will. A better idea for significant changes is to have a new will drawn.
7. *Probate* is the process that occurs when a court reviews a will, confirms its validity, and makes sure that all your creditors of the estate are paid. This is a public process and can be expensive and time consuming.
8. A *living trust* is a document that is used to avoid probate. When combined with a credit shelter trust, it can also substantially decrease your estate taxes.
9. The Federal Government (and some state governments) levies estate taxes. These taxes are applied against the value of your

estate that exceeds the exemption amount. The amount exempt from estate taxes will be more than three million dollars over the next few years as the new tax law is phased in.

10. While it is possible to create your own trust, it is strongly recommended that you use an attorney.

DAY 9 DIARY

I am on my way to my financial breakthrough. Today I . . .

_____

_____

_____

_____

_____

_____

_____

_____

_____

_____

_____

_____

_____

_____

_____

_____

_____

_____

_____

_____

_____

Day 10

Increase Your Income

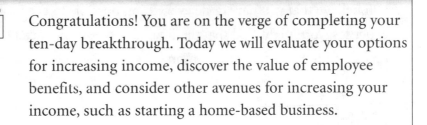

S	M	T	W	T	F	S
	7	8	9	⑩		

☑ Congratulations! You are on the verge of completing your ten-day breakthrough. Today we will evaluate your options for increasing income, discover the value of employee benefits, and consider other avenues for increasing your income, such as starting a home-based business.

WHAT YOU WILL NEED:

- Your family's income figures from current employment.
- A list of benefits that you receive from your employer(s).
- Income figures from any other sources of money your family receives.

INCREASING YOUR INCOME

An area that deserves much more attention than it receives is *income generation*. As mentioned earlier in this book, there are only two ways to

Cashing In

Increasing your income can be a quick method of generating a financial surplus. Consider what an extra $300 per month would be worth: $841,000 in thirty years (at 11 percent interest).

deal with a budget shortfall: Increase income or decrease spending. Almost all of the teaching on the market today focuses on how to cut expenses and live more frugally. An emphasis on this area is extremely legitimate and has been a major theme in this book as well. What I find remarkable is how little focus is placed on increasing income. If, after honestly evaluating your circumstances, you believe that you have done everything possible to decrease expenses, you might find that the final key to your financial breakthrough is earning more money.

CHRISTIAN MONEY PRINCIPLE

Finding a means of increasing your income may not be easy, but God will give you the wisdom you need to find the solution. *But if any of you lack wisdom, you should pray to God, who will give it to you; because God gives generously and graciously to all* (James 1:5 TEV).

I have asked my peers why they are not teaching people how to earn more money. The general answer I receive is that financial problems are not income-based, but caused by overspending. The strong view I hear from almost all personal finance writers and speakers is that people are spending too much money. They feel that increasing their income will make no difference. The thinking is that the more a person earns, the more he or she will spend. This narrow viewpoint troubles me. This may be true for people who do not have a financial plan or objective. But when a person is earning extra money within the context of a conscientious financial plan, this is a positive step toward financial freedom.

For example, 100 percent of this extra money could be directed toward debt reduction, funding a child's college education, or financial independence. I am not a proponent of working harder and longer hours just to satisfy materialistic desires, especially if you are married with children. If you are single and want to work three jobs with the purpose of building a solid foundation for your financial future—go for it! In fact, it is my opinion that if more singles would build up their net worth prior to getting married, marriages would generally be more successful. A large percentage of marital failures are directly attributed to financial stress within the family. What a great preparation for marriage to have your finances in order and also have minimal debts.

HOW MUCH IS ENOUGH?

Probably the most difficult issue of all is answering the question, "How much money is enough?" I don't know that there really is a right and wrong answer to this question. What is most often taught within Christian circles is that we should be content with the material possessions that we have. That is true, but does this mean we are to stay forever at the status quo, never attempting to become financially independent? I think not. Paul said, *I have learned the secret of being content in any and every situation, whether well fed or hungry, whether living in plenty or in want* (Philippians 4:12). Paul could have said "I am content being poor *and* in want," but he didn't. His words seem to provide a "Plan B." Still, I struggle with this issue on a daily basis. I know people who live much simpler lifestyles than I do. I also am acquainted with some who live in beach homes worth millions of dollars.

Even among those individuals who tend to promote the idea of living a modest lifestyle, there is no agreement on what "modest" works out to be. For some, having two vehicles would be considered extravagant, while others consider these necessities. We also cannot discount the overall good that wealthy individuals do for our society. These are the people who provide jobs and create wealth for hundreds, even thousands, in their employ. For example, while it is true that Bill Gates is incredibly materially wealthy, he is also responsible for the most unprecedented economic boom in American history. Without the Windows operating system, it is highly unlikely that the computer boom of the '90s would have occurred, nor the explosion of the Internet. What is that contribution worth to society? Has Bill Gates made too much money from his accomplishments? I don't think so. So, how much is enough? I can only leave this up to you as a personal and spiritual matter to resolve for yourself.

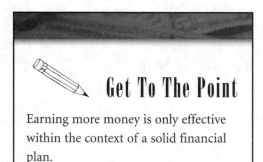

Get To The Point

Earning more money is only effective within the context of a solid financial plan.

If your goal is to balance your budget, why should it matter if part of the solution is found in additional income? Of course, I am the first to agree that if earning more money means sacrificing one's family, it is not a worthwhile tradeoff. On the other hand, there is nothing wrong with a stay-at-home spouse finding a way to make money through a small home-based business. There are countless methods and approaches to be considered. Some people may need to earn additional income for a short period of time (one to two years) until they are able to pay off debts, and then they can easily live on a modest income.

I have received countless calls on the radio shows from single mothers who are earning less than $20,000 per year and cannot make it. It is no wonder! Other people earn additional income to make ends meet and to do those things that the family finds important. Think about it: We are now paying more in taxes than at any time in U.S. history. Earning $50,000 per year is just not what it used to be. After factoring in the cost of a home and one to two vehicles, food, clothing, health care, and other day-to-day expenses, the money just doesn't go very far. The answer in these cases is not to cut expenses. People in these situations need to increase their earnings.

Get To The Point

Earning more money may be your only financial option if your expenses are significantly higher than your income.

COMMON OBSTACLES TO EARNING EXTRA INCOME

- *Lack of Education*—If you're not educated, get educated! People can now earn college degrees in programs designed for working adults and even on the Internet. There are an abundance of

Get To The Point

Anyone can increase their income if they purpose to do so.

computer and medical technician certification programs that can be completed in less than two years. These are professional jobs that pay lucrative salaries. (See the article "How to earn a college degree on the Internet" available at Christian Money Net at www.ChristianMoney.com.)

- *Lack of Opportunity*—Consider moving to an area with more job opportunities.

- *Lack of Extra Time*—If you are a single parent and can't seem to find enough time, start a co-op with other single parents and take turns helping out with each other's children. Start a business from home that will allow you to make money and still stay home with your children. Ask the grandparents to help while you work a night shift. These are just a few ideas.

- *Raises and Promotions are Scarce*—Find a company that will pay you what you are worth.

- *Health Problems*—Make your health a priority. Do you exercise and take vitamins? Are you regularly seeing a doctor for an annual physical? Have you given up tobacco and alcohol use? I have two relatives who are blind and have full-time jobs. I know a local basketball coach who has no legs and works every day without complaint. I personally lost my left eye at the age of five. I don't consider this much of a disability compared to those I just mentioned, but it does require lifestyle changes. Despite my "limitations," I read dozens of books each month, earned a black belt in Tae Kwon Do, and have won several gold medals in martial arts competitions. I have never publicly announced my disability, and I am sure that most people would be shocked to know about it. But if it will motivate you, I am glad to share it. Making your health and lifestyle a priority can have a dramatic effect on your ability to improve your financial condition, and even most permanent physical challenges can be overcome with creative solutions.

A JOB IS MORE THAN JUST A JOB

To evaluate your earnings and what might be necessary to bring in more money, you must give fair value to your current employment

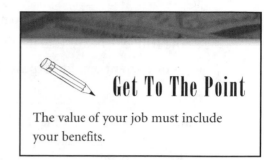

Get To The Point

The value of your job must include your benefits.

benefits. Some employment benefits are priceless. Consider the example of an individual who cannot buy insurance on her own because of a pre-existing medical condition but has employer-provided coverage. Or think about the individuals who have become millionaires because of stock options they have been given as a part of their employment. Whether it is a company retirement plan (especially with matching stock options), insurance benefits, or childcare, you must put a value on the entire package to be able to evaluate your current circumstances accurately.

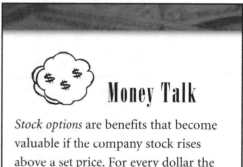

Money Talk

Stock options are benefits that become valuable if the company stock rises above a set price. For every dollar the stock rises above the "strike price" you profit $100 for each option contract you have.

An individual with a large family who receives these important benefits from his employer might have to earn $15,000 more per year than he is currently earning to quit his job and become self-employed. This would include having to pick up his own health insurance costs as well as paying 100 percent of the Social Security tax. (If you work for someone else, the employer pays 50 percent of your Social Security tax.) For many families, it makes sense for at least one person in the household to continue traditional employment, if for no other reason than receiving the fringe benefits. Use the following chart to determine the value of your current employer-provided benefits.

EMPLOYMENT COMPENSATION ANALYSIS

Benefit provided	Economic value

_____ + _____ = _____
Total Value of Benefits   Base Pay   Total Compensation

HOW TO INCREASE YOUR INCOME

Asking for a raise may be the last thing you want to do to earn more money, but it is the most practical in many cases. If you enjoy your job and honestly believe that you want to be there for a long time, it may make

sense to request an increase in pay. While larger companies tend to have a more systematic approach to raises—through processes such as annual reviews—smaller and medium-size companies tend to leave things much more informal. Prior to requesting a meeting with your supervisor, it is important to do some preparation. First of all, compile a list of all of the tasks that you are responsible for on a daily basis. Many employers have no idea just what their employees actually do during the course of a day. Then, continue adding to your list additional responsibilities you would be willing to take on for additional pay. Also, use the Internet to research what the going pay rate is for your occupation within your area.

Now you are ready to ask for a meeting with your supervisor. I would take not more than thirty minutes to discuss your request. It is important that you present all of your facts: What you are doing for the company, what you would be willing to add to your workload, and how much of an increase in pay you are requesting. It is critically important that you ask for—and not demand—a raise. There is no way to know how your employer will react to your request, so do not present a "take it or leave it" proposition. If you already have another job lined up, you may be in a better bargaining position. (Remember, don't rule out relocating if it means a substantial increase in your income.)

The key is to not get emotionally wrapped up in the whole matter. You may get the raise, and then again you may not. You can always still pursue other options including asking again in a month or two, or quietly looking for another job. Whatever you do, and no matter how tempting it is, do not under any circumstances discuss the matter with coworkers. Nothing would be worse than the whole department hearing that you got a raise. Doing this encourages all of the workers to demand a raise, using your raise as their justification. Needless to say, this would not foster a better relationship between you and your employer.

Get To The Point

Consider additional employment or starting a home-based business.

Adding additional employment within your family might be at least one answer to your immediate financial problems. Consider the following scenarios:

- A single person could work two full-time jobs.
- A married individual could work one full-time job and one part time job.
- A married couple could each work one full-time job.
- A married couple could each work one full-time job, while one partner works a second part-time job.
- A stay-at-home spouse could start a business or get a job that is done from home. This is becoming more and more popular. In fact, one of the most valuable members of my organization works for me 100 percent from home.
- A single person could start a full-time home business that can be done in addition to a traditional full-time job.

- A married person could start a part-time home business and work the business at night and on weekends.
- A married couple could start a home business together and even involve the children in the enterprise.

I do not believe that any of these scenarios are impossible. It is important to keep in mind that you may only need this additional income for a relatively short period of time if you use it for the purpose of accomplishing your goals in the area of debt and investing.

There are hundreds of simple businesses that can be completely started and run from home. For most families, just a few hundred dollars extra each month is all that they need to close the gap. There are dozens of books available that are packed with ideas for home-based businesses. For ideas and help in starting your own business, call my office at 800-373-7115.

There are a large number of work-at-home scams that have been around for years. Many involve assembly work or stuffing envelopes

Get To The Point

Be very cautious with popular work-at-home ads for income.

and require you to pay a substantial fee in advance to "qualify" for the work. Before getting involved with any such business opportunity, you should thoroughly check out the company by contacting the Better Business Bureau and the attorney general in the state where the company's main office is located.

The requirement of an investment to get involved in a business is not necessarily a problem, but if you are having immediate cash flow problems, you should look for a low-cost start up. Other sources of good ideas are the small business magazines that you will find at your local bookstore. *Entrepreneur* magazine even sells a series of manuals on how to start various businesses. I have purchased some of these manuals, and they are very well written with complete details and step-by-step instructions. Use common sense, though, since many times the magazines contain the kinds of "opportunities" I have warned you about. Check out *any* company before you do business with them.

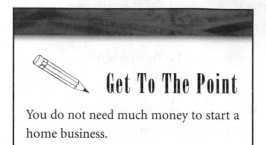

Get To The Point

You do not need much money to start a home business.

The amount of capital your home-based business will require will depend on the business you select. Businesses that tend to require less capital are service businesses. For example, you could start an appointment-setting service for local insurance agents. All that would be required is a telephone and a list of their sales prospects. Another easy business to start is a cleaning service. Cleaning a local office in your neighborhood could pay several hundred dollars per month and only require a vacuum cleaner and about $20 in cleaning supplies (plus elbow grease).

CHOOSING THE RIGHT HOME BUSINESS

I would suggest that in the beginning of your pursuit to earn extra money, you be as practical as possible. If you don't have the capital to start a more expensive enterprise, then find one you can afford now. You can always move on to something different in the future. You may even be able to sell your business at that time or hire someone to do the work and still keep a portion of the profits. The point is not to get consumed with the decision—you don't have to stick with it for the rest of your life.

Many people discover their ideal business in a hobby or other avocation. While I was growing up, my mother sold macramé and made a good amount of money doing something that she absolutely loved. Perhaps you will find the idea for your home-based business in this same manner.

HOW EXTRA INCOME CAN AFFECT YOUR FINANCIAL FUTURE

What if you started a home-based business and earned $500 per month? How could this $500 be used to improve your financial health?

- $500 per month invested in the stock market averaging 11 percent per year would be worth $227,000 in just 15 years!
- $500 per month would pay off a $10,000 credit card balance at an 18 percent interest rate in just 24 months!
- If you had a 15-year mortgage for $150,000 with an 8 percent interest rate and you paid an extra $500 per month, you would pay off the entire mortgage in only nine years!

 **INTERNET TIME SAVERS**

Freelance Job Search Sites

www.elance.com

www.freeagent.com

www.guru.com

www.talentmarket.com

www.talentmarket.monster.com

Job Search Sites

www.ajb.dni.us—America's Job bank

www.careermosaic.com

www.careerpath.com

www.careers.wsj.com

www.careers2000.com

www.dice.com

www.hotjobs.com

www.isleuth.com/empl.html

www.job-hunt.org

www.joboptions.com

www.jobtrak.com

www.jobweb.com

www.jumpstartyourjobsearch.com

www.myjobsearch.com

www.nationjob.com

www.net-temps.com

Free Internet Provider Service

www.netzero.com

FAST TRACK

1. For many people, *part* of their financial solution is increasing income.

2. Before assuming that you have an income problem, live on a budget with a specific spending plan for a period of time.

3. Increasing your income can occur from additional employment and also from owning your own business. There are several scenarios that you should consider: Taking on a part-time or additional full-time job, or starting at least one home-based part-time business.

4. It makes no sense to strive to earn more money just to increase your social status or to accumulate unneeded luxuries. If, on the other hand, you are increasing your income to pay off debt and/or invest toward your financial independence, that makes it a worthy pursuit.

5. If necessary, consider going back to school. You can even earn your college degree completely over the Internet. If you have a low income, you should check out scholarships, grants, and other funding options that are available. You will find these services and links at www.tenday.com. You will also find an article entitled "How to Earn Your College Degree Over the Internet" inside Christian Money Net (www.christianmoney.com/moneynet.htm).

6. It is important to consider the value of the benefits associated with your employment. This is not just a consideration if you decide to go out on your own and start a business, but also to make accurate comparisons if you are job shopping. For example, a low-paying job with great benefits may be your best choice if you have a child that has significant medical expenses.

7. Consider asking for a raise from your current employer. If he or she says no, inquire as to what you might do to be eligible for a raise. It might mean taking on more work or even going back to school. Most employers will let you know if there are any options like this. Many companies will even pay for an employee's education if it is work related.

8. Stay away from "scam" work-from-home opportunities such as stuffing envelopes or assembly work. These ads usually ask for you to send money in advance. Check out any work-from-home opportunity with your state attorney general or the Better Business Bureau prior to making a decision or sending any money.

DAY 10 DIARY

I have now completed all of the steps for my financial breakthrough.
Today I . . .

_____

_____

_____

_____

_____

_____

_____

_____

_____

_____

_____

_____

_____

_____

_____

_____

_____

_____

Sustaining Your Breakthrough

Now that you have completed your *10-Day Financial Breakthrough,* you are among the distinct minority of Americans who have direction for their financial future. You have undoubtedly saved hundreds—if not thousands—of dollars in your annual expenses. What's even more exciting is that you now have specific financial goals and a detailed plan. You are on your way to reaching them! Are you finished? No. In order to continue enjoying the benefits of *The 10-Day Financial Breakthrough,* you need to periodically check your progress and make adjustments along the way. To that end, I am providing you with the following annual financial maintenance schedule. Of course, you should continually be aware of your financial circumstances, be sure that you are living within your budget, and fund your "Automatic Wealth" plans as well. Use the following schedule to review each step of your financial breakthrough.

Sustaining Your 10-Day Financial Breakthrough

January	Goals
February	Budgeting
March	Investing
April	Debt
May	Taxes
June	Goals (Yes, its worth doing twice a year.)
July	Life and Health Insurance
August	Auto, Homeowner's, and Liability insurance

September	Estate Planning
October	Income
November	Credit (A good time to review before a Christmas spending spree)
December	Ok, you get a break for Christmas, but only if you agree not to overspend!

Appendix A

NO-LOAD MUTUAL FUNDS

Note: For a more complete, up-to-date list, check out the Web site: www.ChristianMoney.com.

AARP
P.O. Box 2540
Boston, MA 02208

(800) 253-2277

ACORN
227 West Monroe, Suite 3000
Chicago, IL 60606

(800) 922-6769

AETNA
151 Farmington Avenue
Hartford, CT 06156

(800) 367-7732

AMERICAN CENTURY FUNDS
4500 Main Street
Kansas City, MO 64111

(800) 345-2021

AMERICAN HERITAGE
1370 Avenue of the Americas
New York, NY 10019

(212) 397-3900

AMERICAN PENSION INVESTORS
P.O. Box 2529
2303 Yorktown Avenue
Lynchburg, VA 24501

(800) 544-6060

ANALYTIC OPTIONED EQUITY
P.O. Box 2798
Boston, MA 02209
(800) 374-2633

BABSON
700 Karnes Blvd.
BMA Tower Bldg.
Kansas City, MO 64108
(800) 422-2766

BARON FUNDS
767 5th Avenue
New York, NY 10153
(800) 992-2766

BARTLETT
36 E. Fourth Street, Suite 400
Cincinnati, OH 45202
(800) 800-4612

BERGER
210 University Boulevard, #900
Denver, CO 80206
(800) 333-1001

BOSTON COMPANY
One Boston Place
Boston, MA 02108
(617) 722-7000

BRANDYWINE
3908 Kennett Pike
Greenville, DE 19807
(302) 656-6200

BULL AND BEAR
11 Hanover Square
New York, NY 10005
(800) 847-4200

CAPSTONE
5847 San Felipe, #4100
Houston, TX 77057
(800) 262-6631

CENTURY SHARES
One Liberty Square
Boston, MA 02109
(800) 321-1928

CGM
222 Berkley Street, Suite 1013
Boston, MA 02116
(800) 345-4048

COLUMBIA
1301 S.W. Fifth Avenue
P.O. Box 1350
Portland, OR 97207
(800) 547-1707

COREFUND
530 E. Swedesford Road
Wayne, PA 19087
(800) 355-2673

CRABBE HUSON
121 S.W. Morrison Street, Suite 1425
Portland, OR 97204
(800) 541-9732

DODGE AND COX
One Sansome Street, 35th Floor
San Francisco, CA 94104
(800) 621-3979

DREYFUS
200 Park Avenue
New York, NY 10166
(800) 645-6561

ECLIPSE
P.O. Box 2196
Peachtree City, GA 30269
(800) 872-2710

EVERGREEN
200 Berkeley St.
Boston, MA 02116
(800) 343-2898

FIDELITY
82 Devonshire Street
Boston, MA 02109
(800) 544-8888

FIRST EAGLE
P.O. Box 182497
Columbus, OH 43218
(800) 451-3623

FLEX
6000 Memorial Drive
P.O. Box 7177
Dublin, OH 43017
(800) 325-3539

FOUNDERS
2930 E. Third Avenue
Denver, CO 80206
(800) 525-2440

FREMONT
50 Fremont Street, Suite 3600
San Francisco, CA 94105
(800) 548-4539

GABELLI
One Corporate Center
Rye, NY 10580
(800) 422-3554

GALAXY
4400 Computer Drive
West Borough, MA 01581
(800) 628-0414

GATEWAY
400 Techne Center Drive, Suite 220
Milford, OH 45150
(800) 354-6339

GINTEL
6 Greenwich Office Park
Greenwich, CT 06831
(800) 243-5808

GRADISON McDONALD
580 Walnut Street
Cincinnati, OH 45202
(800) 869-5999

GREENSPRING
2330 West Joppa Road, Suite 110
Lutherville, MD 21093
(800) 366-3863

HARBOR
One Sea Gate, 13th Floor
Toledo, OH 43666
(800) 422-1050

IAI
3700 First Bank Place
P.O. Box 357
Minneapolis, MN 55440
(800) 945-3863

INVESCO
P.O. Box 173706
Denver, CO 80217
(800) 525-8085

JANUS
100 Fillmore Street, Suite 300
Denver, CO 80206
(800) 525-3713

KAUFMANN
140 E. 45 Street, Floor 43
New York, NY 10017
(800) 261-0555

LEGG MASON
100 Light Street
Baltimore, MD 21297
(800) 822-5544

LEPERCQ-ISTEL
1675 Broadway, 16th Floor
New York, NY 10019
(800) 338-1579

LEXINGTON
Park 80 W. Plaza 2
P.O. Box 1515
Saddle Brook, NJ 07662
(800) 526-0056

LINDNER
7711 Carondelet Avenue, Suite 700
P.O. Box 11208
St. Louis, MO 63105
(314) 727-5305

LOOMIS SAYLES
One Financial Center
Boston, MA 02111
(800) 633-3330

MATHERS
100 Corporate N., Suite 201
Bannockburn, IL 60015
(800) 962-3863

MAXUS
1301 E. 9th Street
Cleveland, OH 44114
(216) 687-1000

MERIDIAN
60 E. Sir Francis Drake Blvd.
Wood Island, Suite 306
Larkspur, CA 94939
(800) 446-6662

MERRIMAN
1200 Westlake Avenue, N.
Seattle, WA 98109
(800) 423-4893

MONETTA
1776-A S. Naperville Road, Suite 207
Wheaton, IL 60187
(800) 666-3882

MONTGOMERY
600 Montgomery Street
San Francisco, CA 94111
(800) 428-1871

MOSAIC MUTUAL FUND
1655 N. Fort Myer Drive
Arlington, VA 22209
(888) 670-3600

NEUBERGER AND BERMAN
605 Third Avenue, 2nd Floor
New York, NY 10158
(800) 877-9700

NEW CENTURY
20 William Street, Suite 330
Wellesley, MA 02181
(617) 239-0445

NICHOLAS
700 N. Water Street, Suite 1010
Milwaukee, WI 53202
(800) 227-5987

NORTHEAST INVESTORS
50 Congress Street
Boston, MA 02109
(800) 225-6704

OAKMARK
Two N. LaSalle Street
Chicago, IL 60602
(800) 476-9625

OBERWEIS
951 Icecream Drive, Suite 200
North Aurora, IL 60542
(800) 323-6166

PACIFICA
230 Park Avenue
New York, NY 10169
(800) 662-8417

PAX World Fund
222 State Street
Portsmouth, NH 03801
(800) 767-1729

PERMANENT
P.O. Box 5847
Austin, TX 78763
(800) 531-5142

PERRITT
120 S. Riverside Plaza, Suite 1745
2038 Tower Offices
Chicago, IL 60606
(800) 338-1579

PRIMARY
First Financial Centre
700 N. Water Street
Milwaukee, WI 53202
(800) 443-6544

PRUDENT SPECULATOR
P.O. Box 75231
Los Angeles, CA 90075
(800) 444-4778

REICH AND TANG
600 5th Avenue, 9th Floor
New York, NY 10020
(212) 830-5225

REYNOLDS
Wood Island, 3rd Floor
80 E. Sir Francis Drake Boulevard
Larkspur, CA 94939
(800) 773-9665

RIGHTIME
Forst Pavilion
218 Glenside Avenue
Wyncote, PA 19095
(800) 242-1421

ROBERTSON STEPHENS
555 California Street, Suite 2600
San Francisco, CA 94104
(800) 766-3863

ROYCE
1414 Avenue of the Americas
New York, NY 10019
(800) 221-4268

RUSHMORE

4922 Fairmont Avenue

Bethesda, MD 20814

(800) 622-1386

SAFECO

P.O. Box 34890

Seattle, WA 98124

(800) 426-6730

SALOMONSMITHBARNEY

One New York Plaza

New York, NY 10004

(800) 445-6529

SBSF

45 Rockefeller Plaza, 33rd Floor

New York, NY 10111

(800) 422-7273

SCHAFER

645 5th Avenue, 7th Floor

New York, NY 10022

(800) 644-6595

SCHRODER

787 Seventh Avenue

New York, NY 10019

(800) 344-8332

SCHWAB

101 Montgomery Street

San Francisco, CA 94104

(800) 435-4000

SCUDDER FUNDS
2 International Place
Boston, MA 02110
(800) 225-2470

SENTRY
1800 N. Point Drive
Stevens Point, WI 54481
(800) 533-7827

SHERMAN, DEAN
60601 N.W. Expressway, Suite 465
San Antonio, TX 78201
(210) 492-1488

SIT
4600 Norwest Center
Minneapolis, MN 55402
(800) 332-5580

SOUND SHORE
P.O. Box 1810
8 Sound Shore Drive
Greenwich, CT 06838
(800) 551-1980

STEINROE
1 South Wacker Drive, 32nd Floor
Chicago, IL 60606
(800) 338-2550

STRATTON
610 W. Germantown Pike, Suite 361
Plymouth Meeting, PA 19462
(800) 634-5726

STRONG
P.O. Box 2936
Milwaukee, WI 53201
(800) 368-3863

SWRW
300 Main Street
Cincinnati, OH 45202
(513) 621-2875

T. ROWE PRICE
10090 Red Run Boulevard
Owings Mills, MD 21117
(800) 638-5660

TWENTIETH CENTURY
P.O. Box 419200
Kansas City, MO 64141
(800) 345-2021

USAA
USAA Building
San Antonio, TX 78288
(800) 531-8181

US Global Investors
P.O. Box 781234
San Antonio, TX 78278
(800) 873-8637

VALUE LINE
711 Third Avenue
New York, NY 10017
(800) 223-0818

VANGUARD
Vanguard Financial Center
P.O. Box 2600
Valley Forge, PA 19482
(800) 662-7447

VISTA
P.O. Box 419392
Kansas City, MO 64141
(800) 348-4782

WARBURG-PINCUS
466 Lexington Avenue, 10th Floor
New York, NY 10017
(800) 888-6878

WAYNE HUMMER
300 S. Wacker Drive, Suite 500
Chicago, IL 60606
(800) 621-4477

WILLIAM BLAIR
222 W. Adams Street
Chicago, IL 60606
(800) 742-7272

WP
One New York Plaza, 30th Floor
New York, NY 10004
(800) 223-3332

WRIGHT INVESTORS SERVICE
1000 LaFayette Boulevard
Bridgeport, CT 06604

Appendix B

COMPLETE INTERNET LIST

www.accuquote.com

www.ajb.dni.us

www.ambest.com

www.americancentury.com

www.ameritrade.com

www.attorneyfind.com

www.bankrate.com

www.better-investing.org

www.careermosaic.com

www.careerpath.com

www.careers.wsj.com

www.careers2000.com

www.cheapskatemonthly.com

www.christianmoney.com

www.collegesavings.org

www.creditreport-net.com

www.creditscoring.com

www.crown.org

www.daveramsey.com

www.dca.org

www.dice.com

www.dripcentral.com

www.ehealthinsurance.com

www.elance.com

www.eloan.com

www.equifax.com

www.estrong.com

www.experian.com

www.fidelity.com

www.financenter.com

www.freeagent.com

www.freecreditreport.com

www.freeedgar.com

www.gomez.com

www.guru.com

www.hotjobs.com

www.hsh.com

www.iiin.com

www.insweb.com

www.invesco.com

www.irs.com

www.irs.gov

www.isleuth.com/empl.html

www.job-hunt.org

www.joboptions.com

www.jobtrak.com

www.jobweb.com

www.jumpstartyourjobsearch.com

www.kiplinger.com

www.lawinfo.com

www.lawyers.com

www.legalopinion.com

www.lendingtree.com

www.smartmoney.com

www.money.com

www.moneycentral.com

www.myjobsearch.com

www.nationjob.com

www.netstockdirect.com

www.net-temps.com

www.netzero.com

www.nodebtnews.com

www.nolo.com

www.prepaidlegal.com

www.quicken.com

www.quicken.com.saving.debt

www.quickquote.com

www.quotesmith.com

www.quotesusa.com

www.scudder.com

www.selectquote.com

www.shareware.com

www.ssa.gov

www.talentmarket.com

www.talentmarket.monster.com

www.taxhelpon-line.com

www.taxsites.com

www.tenday.com

www.tuc.com

www.valueline.com

www.vanguard.com

www.waterhouse.com

www.wsrn.com

About the Author

James L. Paris is the author of more than twenty books on personal finance. He has advised professional athletes, celebrities, broadcast networks, non-profit organizations, and currently manages money for clients in more than forty states. He appears as a financial expert on more than one hundred radio and television programs each year. He has appeared on the Fox News Channel, *The 700 Club*, USA Radio Network, Daystar Television, The Christian Television Network, and countless other nationwide programs. He created and manages Christianmoney.com, a web site designed to help Christians with their finances. He also serves as the President and CEO of five financial services companies that he has founded.

Jim is a graduate of the College for Financial Planning and is licensed as a General Securities Principal with the National Association of Securities Dealers.

Additional copies of this book and other titles by RiverOak Publishing
are available from your local bookstore.

If you have enjoyed this book, or if it has impacted your life,
we would like to hear from you. Please contact us at:

RiverOak Publishing
Department E
P.O. Box 700143
Tulsa, Oklahoma 74170-0143
Or by e-mail at info@riveroakpublishing.com

RIVER
OAK
PUBLISHING